MW00817725

Therapists
Are Human Too
THE HEALING JOURNEY
OF RECIPROCITY

9 Therapists' Personal Stories

JENNIFER NAGEL

*In Collaboration with Shelley J. Cook, Corrinna Douglas,
Dr. Madeleine De Little, Nancy M. Gordon, Lyla Harman,
Tami Blackwell Jennings, Bonnie Lee, and Dr. Rick Miners*

in·fluence
PARTNERS IN PUBLISHING

Published by Grace in Chaos Publications
in partnership with Influence Publishing Inc., 2023
ISBN: 978-1-7753084-2-3

Copyright © 2023 Jennifer Nagel
All rights reserved. No part of this publication may be reproduced, stored in or introduced into a retrieval system, or transmitted, in any form, or by any means (electronic, mechanical, photocopying, recording or otherwise) without the prior written permission of the publisher. This book is sold subject to the condition that it shall not, by way of trade or otherwise, be lent, resold, hired out, or otherwise circulated without the publisher's prior consent in any form of binding or cover other than that in which it is published and without a similar condition including this condition being imposed on the subsequent purchaser.

Copyediting: Erin Della Mattia and Danielle Anderson
Proofreading: Lee Robinson
Front Cover Artwork: gonin/iStockPhoto.com and Jennifer Nagel
Cover Design: Andrew Croft
Typesetting: Tara Eymundson

DISCLAIMER: This book is a personal work of non-fiction. Some of the names and identifying details have been changed to protect the privacy of individuals. Readers of this publication agree that neither Jennifer Nagel nor her publisher will be held responsible or liable for damages that may be alleged as resulting directly or indirectly from the use of this publication. Neither the publisher nor the author(s) can be held accountable for the information provided by, or actions resulting from, accessing these resources. This book is not intended in any way to replace professional healthcare or mental health advice, but to support it.

Author's Note

By Jennifer Nagel

This is a book about how we change and are changed in relationship with others. The relationships each of us write about here are between therapists and clients, between social workers and community members, and our personal relationships with family and friends. In some of these chapters, the author has gone to great lengths to disguise identities and any recognizable details. In some instances, materials and scenarios from a few clients or community members have been attributed to one. Written permission was attained from some of the people mentioned specifically and all have given their blessing for the greater intentions of the message of this book.

A note on terminology: Those who access services for therapy, mental health, and wellness are referred to in various ways, often as "clients," "patients," or "community members." These terms do not fully capture the essence of these relationships between us (the authors in this book) and the people we each work with. You may see different terms in different chapters, but they all imply the nature of the sacred relationship between therapist/social worker and the people they work with.

Dedication

This book is dedicated to all the clients, patients, community members, and others who have inspired and influenced us in ways that you may not realize. Thank you for your courage to ask for help, for your trust, your vulnerability, and your willingness to venture into the unknown so as to become more fully known along your healing journey. We honour you with love, respect, and gratitude.

Testimonials

The therapist-client relationship is a two-way street in which learning happens on both ends. The therapist is a guide who assists the client in their growth, while the client also becomes a part of the therapist's growth. In this outstanding collaborative book, several therapists share their experiences of counselling, the reciprocity of the therapeutic relationship, and how this dynamic has impacted their professional and personal lives. A commitment to health, healing, and lifelong learning is woven through each compelling story. The book is not only fascinating, but it also sheds light on the importance of therapy and why it is time to reframe the counselling experience and remove any barriers or stigmas attached with mental health services.

Alyson Jones, MA, RCC-ACS
CTV mental health expert

* * *

Therapists Are Human Too *is unique in that it shifts the focus to the practitioner and highlights our common humanity—that we are all on this journey of healing, discovery, and growth together. I was deeply moved by the sincerity, depth, genuineness, openness, and insightfulness of each author. I hope reading each chapter will inspire you also.*

Dr. John Banmen, R.Psych.
Co-author, *The Satir Model: Family Therapy and Beyond*

* * *

The opportunity to see self in others is a profound gift. This book is a testament to the equality of the human journey as we share our inner stories. It reveals refreshing, enlightening stories that will warm your heart and open your mind to what can be.

Leona Gallant, Métis Elder
Trainer of the Virginia Satir Developmental Model

* * *

This book offers a unique perspective on the lesser-known side of therapy. Through its pages, therapists' stories weave a tapestry of shared growth and healing—the sacred dance between therapist and client, resonating with mutual transformation and healing that flows in both directions. Therapists Are Human Too *stands as a heartfelt tribute to our collective journey toward healing and the interconnected bonds that bind us all.*

Merissa Jennings-Turner
Therapist/Conscious Film Maker
www.thriveasone.ca

Table of Contents

Acknowledgments

There are so many amazing people who have had an influence on the co-creation of this book, and the circles of influence go far beyond those who are named here. The truth is, each person mentioned has their own circle of influence that has impacted who they are in the world and what they each brought to this book project.

Thank you to Julie Ann for seeing the potential and vision of co-leading a collaborative book writing retreat with me right from the start of our brainstorming—no, *heart-storming*—together. I appreciate your vision, your wisdom, and the unique skills you bring to helping people get their stories out. It has been a joy to work on this project with you.

To each of the courageous authors who joined me on this collaborative writing adventure: thank you from the depths of my heart and soul. I am humbled and amazed by each one of you for sharing yourselves with so much strength in your vulnerability and authenticity. I have so much gratitude for having you in my life and for your contribution to this book.

To the spouses, partners, children, family, and community who supported each of the authors to participate in the collaborative process of writing this book: gratitude and thanks for your blessings and support on this journey.

Thank you to Danielle Anderson, managing editor, for overseeing the editing process as a whole and for being available to share your input and ideas when needed. To Erin Della Matia, editor extraordinaire: your insight, curiosity, and wisdom allowed our stories to fully blossom and bloom onto these pages. I am grateful for the way you worked your magic with each author, editing every chapter and working so collaboratively with each one of them. You have a wonderful gift for amplifying each unique voice to allow the telling of their stories. Erin and Danielle, you are truly a phenomenal editing team!

To the rest of the fabulous Influence Publishing team, including Lee Robinson for your thorough eye in proofreading the manuscript, Tara Eymundson for your typesetting and interior design, and Andrew Croft for your beautiful work on the cover design: I am so grateful for your part in bringing this book into world.

To Lisa Archibald, thank you for the fun and fabulous photo shoot on the rooftop of Casa de Influencia with the authors who were present at the retreat.

To Anita Voth, your organizational and administrative skills were a godsend for keeping us on task. I'm a big fan of checklists and appreciated the thoroughness of each one you sent my way (along with the joy of checking off each item as they were completed). Thank you!

And finally to you, dear reader, a huge thank you for choosing to pick up this book and take this journey with us.

Preface:
The Story of Our
Collaborative Writing Process

By Jennifer Nagel

The idea for this book came into being while on the beach at Banderas Bay in Puerto Vallarta, Mexico. Along with several others who lead programs and workshops, I had been invited to visit the newly renovated Casa de Influencia to experience and envision possibilities for future programs and retreats. Standing in a circle out in the water with this small group which included the founder of Influence Publishing, Julie Ann (who had been very involved in the publishing of my first book several years ago), we shared ideas and dreamed about what might be possible for retreats in collaboration with others. For myself, I knew that the people I hoped to gather together for retreats would be mental health and wellness professionals who were looking for opportunities for their own personal and professional growth.

The idea of working on a collaborative book was not a new one, but the idea of holding a week-long retreat where all the authors would come together in a space of shared energy and support and complete the first draft of their book chapter in that week—now *that* was new! Julie Ann and I both had goosebumps of excitement as we discussed this shared vision of collaboration. Working together seemed like a natural fit—she with her multitude of gifts for bringing out people's stories, along with her editing and publishing team, and I with my passion for and experience with building safety, connection, community, and depth of process for groups, along with both of our personal experiences with writing. Thus began our collaboration for manifesting this vision into reality.

It's amazing how the sharing of ideas with one another catapulted and contributed to the development of the theme for this book. What initially began as an exploration of how the work of therapists impacts their clients turned into a captivating question of how the clients' personal journeys of healing—their shifts and transformations—have impacted their therapists: What have therapists learned from and with their clients that has helped them in their own personal lives?

Reciprocity in therapeutic relationships has been a theme for myself as well as for the therapists for whom I provide clinical supervision. We often find ourselves reflecting on what we learn from and with our clients through the process of working with them. As a clinical supervisor, a big focus of the work I do with other therapists is on *the person of the therapist*: by discussing what we experience as we work with our clients, we create space to be curious about what might be going on when certain clients or themes seem to activate reactions within ourselves. Then we can explore the parallels between our clients' lives and our own personal lives. Developing an awareness of how clients can impact the therapist creates opportunities for the therapist to work through their own personal, unfinished business, which results in their being more present and congruent with themselves and their clients.

The concept of reciprocity in therapeutic relationships—all the ways the therapist learns and grows from their clients while clients learn and grow from the work they do with the therapist—led to the idea of bringing together a group of therapists to share their own personal stories of reciprocity. I wanted to gather the diverse stories of therapists and clinical supervisors between the covers of a book to show how, collectively, our lives are impacted by our work with our clients.

Sharing the word about this project and the collaborative writing retreat through personal emails, social media posts, and invitations for online information sessions led to applications from several therapists and helping professionals, each contributing their unique stories. The authors in this book each had their own journeys to the "Yes" that resonated within them at the idea of sharing their stories of reciprocity in a printed (and very public) form. We each come from a variety of places geographically—Vancouver, Kamloops, Parksville, Cowichan Valley, Alert Bay, Oklahoma, San Diego—and a variety of cultures and backgrounds. All are in the profession of helping others. Two of the authors were unable to travel to Mexico to join the writing retreat in person, but their passion and determination to contribute to this project led them to find their own ways to participate, and we found creative ways to include them in the process (thanks in no small part to technology and Zoom).

During our week-long retreat, we laughed, we cried, we held space for one another—brave, authentic, vulnerable, loving, and compassionate space. The courage of each author to tell their story and dive into focused writing in a retreat space resulted in a very full range of chaos, serenity, peace, surrender, and joy. We were supported in this journey by the beautiful surroundings of the area—historical hills of cobblestone streets, flowers and foliage, trees, beaches, water, and ocean breezes. We were nourished by fresh, local food so lovingly prepared for us, and we were inspired by processes that supported the connection, safety, and trust of the group. I believe the depths we each went to in this setting had a profound influence on the personal stories written by each author. We experienced reciprocity in real time as we inspired, encouraged, leaned on, and supported one another to get our stories out. I am grateful to each of the authors in this book for their contributions and their courage to be vulnerable and show up with raw, brave, inspiring authenticity.

Introduction

By Jennifer Nagel

*Abundance is a dance with reciprocity
—what we can give, what we can share,
and what we receive in the process.*

— Terry Tempest Williams

Introduction

By Jennifer Nagel

Helping others and being of service are values that were deeply instilled in me early in life. This contributed to my sense of purpose and ability to form meaningful connections with others. Whether it be giving directions to someone who is lost, listening to the grocery clerk at the checkout line share their concerns about their ailing parent, or just spending time sitting in presence with a dear friend who is grieving a loss, I am touched when others feel I am safe to approach and open up to. Each interaction is a deeper level of intimacy than chitchat about the weather or the latest news. It is a chance to connect us both to our common humanity.

Going into the counselling profession seemed like a natural progression that fit my love for and curiosity about people and my desire to help. What I hadn't realized at the time was just how much I would learn and grow from the therapy sessions I have with the clients who venture through the doors of my office. Their courage to show up and be vulnerable, to hope for healing and lasting change from the pain of whatever they are facing—whether it be physical, psychological, social, or spiritual—continues to impact me for the better. In their sharing and journeying with me, my clients enhance my own journey of growth and healing.

Therapy is not a one-way process. Research tells us the therapeutic relationship is what determines the depth of the work. This relationship involves a dynamic equilibrium of interactions and exchanges between therapist and client where we respond to and witness each other. Both contribute to and receive from the relationship. Both affect and are affected by the other. We are equal in value no matter what our role is in the relationship.

Underneath the roles of "therapist" and "client" lies the very fact that we are all human beings. Yes, therapists are human too, and we all have unique human experiences of loss, grief, trauma, adventure, joy, and so on. Therefore, as our clients entrust themselves to the therapeutic relationship and do the work of healing, we the therapists also bring to the process our own life experiences which we are continuing to learn and grow from. Growth is a lifelong process; after all, we don't just reach an end point where we say, "Yup, I'm finished growing now." The very interaction between any two or more people in community will have an impact on whoever and whatever is involved in the interaction. Giving and receiving, receiving and giving—*this is the dynamic of reciprocity.*

There are times when the processes we have journeyed through with our clients end up being the very medicine we need ourselves. An uncanny cluster of themes will present themselves and end up being for the therapist's own learning and growth, whether the client's experiences are parallel to something the therapist is currently going through or something not yet known to the therapist (which in hindsight becomes somewhat of a premonition, one could say).

When I was diagnosed with multiple sclerosis the month before my fiftieth birthday, I had a roller coaster of emotions and thoughts. It was not quite the birthday gift I was hoping for! However, in some ways, it was possibly the very gift I needed, although I certainly didn't see it that way in the beginning. The MRI scans showing multiple lesions in my brain terrified me. I felt frustrated when my walking and thinking were challenged by too much heat, fatigue, and stress. I panicked about who I would be if I couldn't use my brain "properly" for processing and communicating.

And then an epiphany came to me—a reminder of some of the clients I had accompanied through their own journeys with brain injuries from accidents, illnesses, or other traumas. A reminder of that "cluster of themes" I was just referring to—the work each client and I had done together to transform the relationship with their body, with their brain, to have more love and compassion for self, learning to listen to the wisdom of their body. *Ah,* I thought to myself, *so THIS is the work I need to do with ME now.* Acknowledging and accepting the diagnosis, allowing space for the varying emotions of grief about the way things were in the past. Practicing mindfulness and meditation to connect with the essence of who I am underneath the diagnosis and limitations—limitless possibilities within limits. Witnessing and being with my clients as they cultivate gratitude and appreciation for all the ways their bodies are continuing to support their life—the breath, the heartbeat, the blood cells flowing throughout the body, the miracle of it all.

Looking at the bigger picture while being connected with gratitude and other internal resources that were in the service of Life allowed my clients—and therefore me—to listen to the wisdom of what else our bodies wanted to say. *This* was the medicine that served me so beautifully as I continued my own journey of accepting, having gratitude for, and honouring the gifts that MS was here to teach me. My clients had paved the way for me to put into practice the very things we had worked on together.

* * *

Each of us emerges as a bud on a universal spiritual tree. That tree links all human beings through its roots. Each of us can learn how to become a wise leader who will love, take care of, and nurture the precious life we have been given. When we ourselves have been nourished, we can then be appropriate in our nourishment of others.

— Virginia Satir

There is a multi-dimensional dance of energy happening in the sacred space of therapy. How I am with myself and how I am with my client interplays with how my client is with themselves and how they are with me. I desire for my clients to experience *me* seeing *them*, and for them to experience themselves mirrored back—the beautiful and resourceful essence and soul of who they truly are underneath the coping, pain, and old patterns of survival.

Awareness of what each person brings to the relationship allows for more conscious and intentional co-creation through the therapy process. The way the therapist shows up and is present in body, mind, and spirit in the presence of their clients and group members allows for safety, trust, and connection to be established. I have my own internalized relationship with myself: how I experience myself in any moment through my actions, my energy, my bodily sensations, my emotions, my beliefs and thoughts, my expectations, and my yearnings. I have varying levels of awareness and connection with my gifts of intuition, creativity, wisdom, and holding space for myself and others. My clients also have their own internalized relationship with themselves in any moment, with varying awareness of the influence of actions and events on their energy, bodily sensations, feelings, beliefs and perceptions, expectations, and yearnings. We each have our own personal experience of our relationship with the other which could be a very different, subjective experience for each. Each client is unique in their life experiences and how they react and respond to these experiences, resulting in every relationship I have being unique. Therefore, there is no cookie-cutter approach when it comes to therapy, as there is a unique "we" energy (consisting of multiple energies) that exists between any two people. However, at the core essence of our *Being*, we *are* the same. We have the same yearnings for safety and love, and the same access to internal resources for healing and growth. Knowing this at an energetic level allows me to connect more deeply with each client and for them to connect more deeply with themselves and their own wisdom, intuition, and abilities for healing and growth.

The processes that emerge from being in presence with one another, the information that I receive verbally, nonverbally, intuitively, and through all senses, allows for the co-creation of the path toward healing as clients do the work of letting go, adding in, reconnecting, repairing, and resolving—transforming their old ways of being to become more fully their true selves. As clients awaken to themselves and their capacity to take more responsibility for creating their experience rather than remaining in their suffering, I am also impacted. I feel my own energy resonating and expanding as I experience gratitude and awe for what becomes possible in the sacred space of the therapeutic relationship. This goes beyond helping the people I work with in therapy and enters the realm of fueling my hopes for what is possible not only in my personal relationships but also for humanity.

The very fact that our clients show up and walk through the door (even if they say they "had no choice") tells me there is a part of them, no matter how big or small, that holds hope for change—that something could be different. They just do not yet know how that might be possible. I believe that when someone shows up for an appointment, even if that person has been mandated to attend, they have still made a choice to be there and sit in front of me. An essential part of the therapeutic relationship is holding hope for our clients and connecting them with their own hope. By holding this hope, the therapist opens the doors for the client to gain more awareness and choice of how they respond in the world with themselves, others, and all that Life presents along the journey.

I have learned so much from journeying alongside my clients in their willingness to go to the depths and explore inward, discover the gems of wisdom within, and realize their own life energy that moves them forward toward healing. It is powerful to be with clients as they gather courage to feel all their feelings, express them, and navigate the walls of protection that have served their purpose but may no longer be needed. I am truly honoured to venture into the deep shadows and lovingly bring out the light of compassion to nurture the hidden parts of people that yearn to be seen.

What I receive from my clients contributes to my experience of feeling deeply in touch with humanity in all its complexity, as well as the simplicity of its common foundation. Every one of us has the same yearnings—yearnings for safety, freedom, love, belonging, connection, and peace. Universal yearnings make us hardwired for connection. This is something I take with me into my life outside of the therapy room.

What I appreciate about this work is that in order to hold a mirror up for my clients, I also take a look at my own self in the mirror. I am called to continually develop my own awareness and acceptance of myself as I am in order to acknowledge what is going on within me, rather than ignore, push away, run away from, or deny it. To do good work in therapy and be fully present with my clients, I need to bring my authenticity into the room.

* * *

Therapists Are Human Too: The Healing Journey of Reciprocity holds stories of authenticity, vulnerability, the process of rising from the ashes and navigating through the journey of being human. Each of the authors in this book has their own unique way of being in the world and helping other people, and this uniqueness is reflected in their stories. In their contributions, the authors share the diverse ways their clients and community members have transformed their own lives. Yet, the stories still share a common ground of heart-based passion for the work we are called to do. Underlying themes emerge as the stories intertwine: promise, forgiveness, intergenerational trauma and healing, and the journey toward more love and compassion for self and others.

There is an interweaving of client, therapist, we-ness, oneness, and the wisdom of the entire collective that contributes to the creation of a beautiful tapestry of our shared humanity—the flow of reciprocity.

The hope for this book is that you, the reader, will find yourself in one or more of these stories and recognize that you are not alone. We all exist in connection with other people, no matter one's predetermined role. Underneath all the hats we wear and the roles we play, we are *all* human beings with the same yearnings for connection, love, acceptance, and so much more. For the therapists and wellness professionals reading this book, we hope you will be inspired to compassionately and courageously connect with your own personal growth journey and vulnerabilities to inform and enhance the way you bring your unique presence to your work. For all readers, we hope to reduce the stigma around reaching out for help and to expand the understanding that there is reciprocity in the process of connection within therapeutic relationships. Perhaps these stories will stimulate your own reflections on the various relationships that have changed and transformed your life. Perhaps they will allow you to make new choices about your healing and growth toward more freedom, self-love, compassion, and alignment with the abundance of who you truly are at your essence.

About Jennifer Nagel

Born in Vancouver, British Columbia, Canada, Jennifer Nagel, MA, RCC, studied Psychology in university and found that the best learning came from life experience and doing the work she is so passionate about. Writing about reciprocity in therapy comes from her first-hand experience of learning from and with the people and communities she works with.

Jennifer is a Registered Clinical Counsellor and works with individuals, couples, and families. She has helped many people on their journeys of learning to show up more authentically in their personal and professional lives. She travels the world and teaches professional and personal growth programs using the Satir Model in Canada, China, Kenya, and Thailand. She works with diverse groups including therapists, educators, school programs, community organizations, at-risk adolescents, therapeutic programs, non-profit organizations, and corporate clients.

Jennifer is a member of the British Columbia Association for Clinical Counsellors and the Virginia Satir Global Network and is a clinical member of the Satir Institute of the Pacific. She is also the Director of Trainer Development for the Satir Institute of the Pacific and a senior faculty member of the Banmen Satir China Management Center. Jennifer works with individuals, couples, and families in private practice, and provides clinical supervision for other therapists. She is the author of *Magic in the Muck: Finding Grace in Chaos*, and a contributing author in *Woman of Worth: Moms in Business* and *Woman of Worth: Pandemic! Stories of Purpose, Passion & Power Through this Extraordinary Era.* Jennifer is passionate about teaching Satir Transformational Systemic Therapy programs around the world.

www.facebook.com/jennifernagelcounselling/
www.linkedin.com/in/jennifernagelcounselling/
www.jennifernagelcounselling.com

1

Bonnie the Therapist Becomes More Human

By Bonnie Lee

There is freedom waiting for you,
On the breezes of the sky,
And you ask "What if I fall?"
Oh but my darling,
What if you fly?

— Erin Hanson

Bonnie the Therapist Becomes More Human

By Bonnie Lee

I walked into the meeting room at Simon Fraser University in Vancouver, Canada. I was very early because I wanted to make sure I got a spot in the back of the room for the Satir Transformational Systemic Therapy (STST) training program I had travelled from Oklahoma to attend. As I passed through the double doors and scanned the room, my stomach clenched and I broke out in a sweat. The room was large and contained little else aside from a circle of about twenty chairs arranged in the middle of the room. A circle. How was I going to hide in the back row in a circle? Panic began to rise in my chest. This was not working out like it was supposed to. To start with, Vancouver was in the midst of a heatwave that rivalled the one hundred-degree temperatures of Oklahoma. I looked on the internet: Vancouver was not supposed to be hot. Further, I was learning that because of the "mild" weather, Vancouver was not air-conditioned! And now, here I was, facing a circle. How could this get worse? Before I could exit the room, other people started to arrive. I was trapped. I quickly sat down in the chair closest to the door for an easy escape, if needed. I plastered on my biggest smile and exchanged "hellos" with the others. Sweat ran down my face. Everyone was so calm, so lovely, so young, so not sweaty. It seemed they all already knew each other. *Maybe*, I thought, *I am in the wrong room.*

Then in walked—no, to my upset stomach and near heat-stroke brain, in *floated* this beautiful woman who introduced herself as our trainer, Jennifer Nagel. My plastered smile froze as I watched her sit down at the opposite end of the room. I. Was. Directly. In. Her. Line. Of. Sight.

* * *

I began my journey of becoming a therapist when I met Jennifer at the STST level one training in Vancouver. I had already completed my Bachelor of Science in Psychology and Masters of Marriage and Family Therapy and Community Counselling. From talented professors and mentors I had learned all about counselling history and theory, ethical standards, and how to build rapport with clients. I was nearly finished with the three thousand supervision hours required for licensure under the expertise and talented teaching of my clinical supervisor. But something … something was missing.

I was employed as a therapist at a domestic violence agency, counselling people who had experienced childhood abuse, sexual trauma, or who were or had been in relationships involving domestic violence. I had a wonderful clinical supervisor who was encouraging and attentive. I was utilizing lots of cognitive behavioural therapy to help clients shift their thoughts, which shifts feelings, which shifts behaviour. It was very logical and effective—most of the time. Then there were the times it just didn't seem to be … enough.

I could get to the "brain" of the matter, but there seemed to be a real need to go deeper in order to help my clients make long-term change. Deeper to *where*, I had no idea. My supervisor kept reminding me of the importance of being who I am in sessions. *Who I am?* What exactly did that mean? I began to experience a great deal of anxiety and unease. Apparently I missed the class in graduate school entitled "Who I Am." I began to feel like an imposter, a fraud. I spoke to other therapists and they all assured me the feeling was completely normal—just part of being a new therapist, something that would subside as I gained experience. It was even written about in the textbooks. Problem solved! But, they didn't get it. I had felt like a fraud my entire life. How could I possibly help other people when I felt this way? I decided more education was the answer.

That was when I found a ten-day level one training program based on the work of Virginia Satir. I had been introduced to her theory in my first course in graduate school, "Theories of Counselling." She was a pioneer in Family Therapy. She believed that people had within themselves the ability to change, to heal, to become more fully who they were created to be. I connected to Satir's work in part because her approach was different. She stressed the importance of play, even for adults. She was active and creative in the therapy room. No lying on the couch for her clients! Plus, she was a woman in a male-dominated profession. She was tall and awkward and kind and intelligent and compassionate and wore polyester and created new ideas about people and their possibilities. *Maybe*, I thought, *I could learn more about the ways she did things and copy her techniques and find that deeper something I was missing.* The training was in Canada, but I had never been out of the United States before. I was terrified. I would need a passport! Canadian money! Airplane tickets! Plus, there was an application that asked me questions about myself and what kind of counsellor I wanted to be and what my strengths and goals were. I wanted to write "I don't know" for every answer! It felt like I was being asked to give information about myself that was certainly no one's business. Especially since I didn't know the answers. The nerve!

I successfully navigated through the new maze of international travel and finally landed in Vancouver. My plan was to sit in the back of the room, take lots of notes, and then fly back to Oklahoma and ask my wonderful clinical supervisor what I should do next.

When I walked into the training room on the first day and found the chairs arranged in a big circle, I wanted to back out of the room and try to figure out who I should call to get back on the plane to go home. Then I decided that would probably cost a lot of money, and I wasn't at all sure how to even get back to the airport, so I quickly devised a plan B.

I sat in the chair furthest from the speaker set-up, closest to the door. I congratulated myself on my quick thinking. The room began to fill with people. To my dismay, my clever plan put me right in Jennifer's line of sight at the opposite end of the room. She looked right at me. Plan C: Don't make eye contact.

As I concentrated on my feet, I heard Jennifer explain that this training was "experiential." I had anticipated this from the little I knew of Satir's work, as well as the application, but I had not realized that "experiential" would mean "participation required." It was going to be a long ten days. I needed a new plan.

Plan D: I would perform my way through the training. Utilizing the character of Bonnie the Therapist, I would participate in a very competent, well-educated manner that would allow me to appear as if I was really participating but not actually expose anything vulnerable or revealing. It would work. I had played versions of this character my entire life. It was so easy. All I had to do was figure out what other people wanted me to do or how they expected me to act and just do those things and act those ways. Over the years I had given brilliant performances of Bonnie the Homeschool Mom, Bonnie the Sunday School Teacher, Bonnie the Country Girl, Bonnie the Comedian, Bonnie the Play Director, and on and on. It was no-fail. Well done, me!

I implemented my brilliant plan. I actually combined Bonnie the Therapist with Bonnie the Comedian in order to present myself as competent but for protection also give everyone a laugh on me when I found myself having no idea of what I was doing. "Having no idea" is the truth about what I was learning. I had never heard or seen anything like this! We were in this circle for twelve hours a day. That might be an exaggeration. Sometimes we were in the space outside of the circle. The point is we were immersed in learning. *Brainwashing*, I thought, *this is brainwashing*. Jennifer would explain a concept, then we were supposed to process the learning. That meant I was supposed to turn to two or three of these strangers and talk about my feelings. My line became: "So, what does everyone think?" If I said it first then everyone else had to talk, and by the time we got to me I would have some kind of profound insight or we would run out of time.

Then there was the practicing. We would take turns being the therapist, the "star" (Satir's word for the client), and the observer. I tried volunteering to be the observer all the time, but clever Jennifer had two helpers who watched to make sure everyone had an "opportunity" to experience each of the roles. The first few days, I sweated and smiled and joked my way through and made it back to my room and cried. Why had I not been satisfied with cognitive behavioural therapy? Why was I torturing myself? Why wasn't Vancouver air-conditioned?!

During a morning session somewhere on the third or fourth day, something happened. Jennifer was conducting our morning meditation. I had become very good at meditating by this point. It was very easy. I closed my eyes, took some deep breaths, and as Jennifer talked, I mentally worked on my to-do list for when I got home, sang the alphabet, recited bits of skits from *Saturday Night Live*, and then listened with a knowing expression as others accepted the invitation to "share their experience." I was with a group of hippies. This was going to make a great story when I got home. On this particular morning, however, I actually tuned in to Jennifer's words. She was telling us to "go inside ourselves and notice what was there." I thought, *I know what's there, guts … lol … funny me*. She said, "See if you can notice that unique place of 'self' that is unlike any other person, and when you find it, allow it to expand and fill your entire being from head to toe." As she spoke, I saw a little white light, like a white stone. *Sleep deprivation*, I thought, *I am hallucinating*. But it was interesting. As she encouraged us to allow this "self" to grow, I felt a rush of electricity through my body. The white stone began to fill my being. I knew I was seeing, feeling, experiencing my soul. Not a version of Bonnie, but the Bonnie as I was created and seen by God. It absolutely took my breath away. I was known, alive, loved, and absolutely beautiful not because of what I was *doing* but because of who I *am*.

I heard Jennifer asking if anyone wanted to share their experience. Share the experience indeed! What had just happened? Had I become a hippie? How could I go back to Oklahoma?! My body shook from head to toe. Sharing was out of the question. I stood up, willed my legs into some kind of walking motion, and left the circle. No one would notice. The nearly six-foot-tall, sobbing, shaking, sweating, stiff-legged walking, red-headed woman certainly would not draw any attention. Jennifer called a break and came over to me and asked if I needed anything. She was looking at me. I looked back, straight into her beautiful brown eyes, and said "Something just happened," and she said, "I know." That's it. "I know." For the first time in my life, I had an awareness, a knowing of Bonnie. Not a character of Bonnie, but the being of Bonnie, and Jennifer was there to say "I know." That's when it all clicked. I realized what being a therapist truly is. It is being with, holding safe space as another person works to discover who they are in this time, this place, this situation. It is not about digging into the details of all the things that have ever happened; it is discovering and appreciating the resources that developed as a result of all those happenings and noticing the ever-present ability to continue to "become." To become as I was created to become.

I didn't tell anyone—sorry, "share my experience." This was too big. How could I say "I saw my soul"? I was probably in a cult now. I wasn't sure this was in line with my Southern Baptist conservative learning. We weren't supposed to see our souls, or meditate, or sit in circles!

The next day, I had an interesting interaction in my small group. (As if it wasn't enough that we were required to participate as one person in a large group—pretty easy to hide there—we also had to work in small groups to "anchor the learning" and increase the hiding difficulty.) A beautiful young woman from my small group came up to me and said, "Bonnie, I got this to use as a focal point during a meditation class I attended a while back. I knew it didn't really belong to me, but I get a sense it does belong to you." She placed a white stone in my hand. My mouth fell open and tears started to flow again. I was seen and I was known, and I was okay. I was also terrified. I did not know how to survive in my Oklahoma world like this, with all of my carefully constructed walls of protection torn down. Without Bonnie the Actor to take over, I would be so vulnerable. Where would I hide? Then suddenly it came. Awareness. All of the roles I used to hide behind were actually true parts of me. My Bonnie-ness, if you will. However, because so much fear and doubt and shame had piled up for so long, for my entire life, I did not realize I was more than the parts. Connecting in that moment with my soul opened up my ability to experience integration of body, mind, and spirit. I already knew how to survive. I was now free to begin to thrive.

I returned to Oklahoma a world-travelling, experientially trained, hippie therapist with a white stone soul. I was now prepared! Imagine my distress when upon my return I saw my first client and felt absolutely, completely lost! What I did before as a therapist didn't really fit anymore, yet I was not confident enough in the skills I had just learned to trust those either. I looked at my beautiful client who was looking to me to tell her what to do about her abusive relationship. Her husband had just been sentenced to several years in prison for violating his parole for a previous domestic violence conviction. "I really thought he had changed," she said. "I don't feel right about divorcing him now that he is in prison."

I took a deep breath and asked, "What would *you* like to do?"

"I have no idea," she said. "I don't even know who I am anymore."

"I know," I said.

"I am afraid," she said.

"I know," I said, "but who you are—your authentic self—is there waiting for you to notice her. Let's see if we can notice her together."

I believe effective therapy is both a science and an art. I had learned a great deal about the science of therapy, and I understood the concept of the importance of the person of the therapist. Satir calls this "the use of Self." As a therapist, when I am fully connected and present, body, mind, and spirit, I am able to engage with clients from a place of authenticity. But, how does that work when the therapist does not have a good sense of who they are as a human? This was the missing piece I had been searching for. Bonnie the Therapist is not who my clients need. Bonnie the Human who has therapy skills is such a better fit.

From Jennifer I learned a new way to start each therapy session, a technique I now use regularly: "What do you need during our time today?" "I don't know" is often the answer for newer clients. Bonnie the Therapist would get all kinds of anxious over that answer. *How am I going to figure out what this client needs and fix it in fifty minutes?* Bonnie the Human knows I can't fix anything for anyone and that's okay. Instead, I know I can be with someone as they work to discover their own solutions. Bonnie who has therapy skills can say "Let's take some breaths together and notice what's happening in your body right now." We breathe together, we notice, and the work begins.

The work of being human, it turns out, is ongoing, hard work! Just like my clients, I can get lost and have to remember how to come back to myself. One day, a client walked into my office and in the course of our conversation said, "I am afraid I might be schizophrenic." They went on to describe their painful experiences with the mental health care system and their reluctance to seek medical treatment. *Wait, wait!* I thought. *Schizophrenia is really serious, and certainly this human needs someone more than me right now!* I felt my spirit begin to push back from this client as my body tensed. The tension of fear moved across my shoulders. I did not know what to do! But then, a new feeling of peace washed over my entire body. Awareness emerged. A person, just like me, needed to be seen, to be heard. They did not need me to do anything. In this moment they needed me to *be*. To be present, to be authentic, to be with them. Might they also eventually need someone with a different expertise? Perhaps. However, on this day, I connected with this client's courage, not unlike my own, that had motivated them to come to my office and, in essence, say, "I don't know who I am, but I'm afraid it's really scary." *I know*, I thought, then leaned in and said to them, "*You* are not schizophrenia. You may be a person who *has* schizophrenia, but that would be an aspect of you, not the identity of you." A connection was made and our work began. Bonnie the Therapist would have never known how to say that. Remember, she got scared! After all, the "correct" thing to say in such a situation is not listed in any textbook. Yet Bonnie the Human, who has knowledge of mental illness and ethical treatment standards, knew just what to say.

What I do is the overflow of who I am. That's true for all humans, but I had it backwards for the majority of my life. What freedom comes with that particular awareness! I had originally set out to learn more about the STST model with the purpose of learning my way to being a therapist. The learning is important, but it is no less important than growth in my body and spirit. We are all made of body, mind, and spirit! This was a powerful revelation for me, and it turns out it is a powerful revelation for the majority of my clients as well. Still, my ongoing journey of being and becoming Bonnie the Human is often difficult. I discovered that the part of myself I thought I knew—my mind—I didn't know very well at all.

For so long, I had carried a mental image of myself as a large head with feet—Bonnie the Actor. The task was to figure out what others needed from me, then I could become that, and then shazam! All would be well. My body and spirit faithfully chugged along, largely ignored by me. My mind learned lots of things and followed the rules. It may seem like that is enough. Except it isn't. Intelligence is an important aspect of my mind, and my brain does a pretty good job of taking in all of the information and understanding it. (Except for math. My brain is *very* unimpressed with most things mathematical and goes there as infrequently as it can get away with.) Yet, as Bonnie the Human I am frequently challenged by the impact of my thoughts about myself. They are nearly as mean to me as math. "*You*," they say, "are fat, ugly, stupid, too tall, too loud, too emotional, and at any given moment probably have bad breath and body odor." I mean really, why even get out of bed! Why would I even *want* to know such a human? So many of my clients experience the knowing of their minds the same way.

I have also struggled with body image most of my life. But I have learned that giving kindness to my body is about appreciating all it does for me. About giving it some of the things it needs. After all, my body—in all of its shapes and sizes—is the container for my mind and spirit. When I reject my body, or any other aspect of myself, I cannot be authentically who I am.

This continuing awareness for myself and for my clients is what calms that fear and the negative thoughts that insist, "You can't do this! People are going to find out you have no idea what you are talking about!" About three years ago, I was standing in front of a large window in my bedroom. I had just had my third round of chemotherapy following a double mastectomy necessitated by a diagnosis of breast cancer. I was scared. I was tired. I was sad. I was *bald*. Good grief! I looked down at myself and in that moment was overwhelmed with gratitude for my body. There it was, with parts of it amputated, poisoned with chemo in order to heal it, and yet, there it stood. Holding me upright so I could look out of the window. After all of the unkindness I had given it all these years, and still do, sometimes…. It's just so easy to forget and fall back into old habits. Fortunately, my clients frequently give me the opportunity to remember.

A client comes to see me and tells me she has depression from a staggering amount of "life" happening all at once. "I know what I need to do," she says, "but I just can't. I feel crazy." I assure her that "crazy" is not a diagnosis—my own little, very humorous reply to this common concern—then I ask her, "How is your sleep?"

"Just terrible," she says. "I haven't slept well in days."

"What about your nutrition? Are you giving your body some of the nutrients it needs?"

She hunches her shoulders forward. "Probably not. Most days I just grab whatever I can, and it's usually crap."

I know, I think. "How about hydration? Are you having some water every day?"

"Well, if Dr. Pepper counts, I'm great there."

We begin to create a plan together. Not an obvious plan to address her depression, but a self-care plan for her body. Sleep, nutrition, and water.

As my client tended to the needs of her body, she began to feel better able to take action on what she came to my office knowing. The body needs sleep, food, hydration. It seems so unbelievably basic, and it is … until we forget, or if no one ever really taught us about it. When we don't give our bodies what they need, our brilliant minds and our beautiful spirits struggle. When we are able to give our bodies what they need, that is when we can begin to thrive in body, mind, and spirit. The seemingly separate parts of us are connected within ourselves. Jennifer taught me that and continues to teach me. I teach the same to my clients, and as I teach, I am reminded of the same for myself. How lovely is that?

About Bonnie Lee

Bonnie Lee, MS, LPC, lives in Owasso, Oklahoma. She earned her Bachelor of Science from Rogers State University in Claremore, Oklahoma, and her Masters of Marriage and Family Therapy and Community Counseling from John Brown University in Siloam Springs, Arkansas. She is level-three trained in Gottman Method Couples Therapy and is also trained in Eye Movement Desensitization and Reprocessing (EMDR). She currently works with first responders and their families as well as running a small private practice.

Bonnie continues her work and training in Satir Transformational Systemic Therapy. She strives to not only utilize the model professionally but to live out the concepts of authenticity and connection with self and others in her personal life. When she is not working, she enjoys spending time with friends and family, reading, and quilting.

yourstoriesmatter23@gmail.com
www.facebook.com/bonnie.l.cagle
www.linkedin.com/in/bonnie-lee-5a5173108/

2

Inspired to Change: Rediscovering Me Through Reflections of Clients' Healing

By Corrinna Douglas

*Owning our story anoving ourselves through
that process is the bravest thing we'll ever do.*

— **Brené Brown**

Inspired to Change: Rediscovering Me Through Reflections of Clients' Healing

By Corrinna Douglas

I opened the door to my office and welcomed Lacey inside. As she settled into our therapeutic space, I intuitively and energetically sensed the sadness and pain on her. I chose to begin our session with a grounding exercise. The guided visual meditation invited Lacey to connect with areas in her body where she may be experiencing tenderness or pain and offer some love with acceptance and compassion. As she did this, tears rolled down her face, and when she opened up her eyes we connected in a loving sacred energy that gave her permission to release more tears. She said, "Thank you, thank you for seeing me."

After that experience, I started to realize that my private practice was welcoming a vast number of new clients whose stories resonated with Lacey's struggle. Stories about guilt, placating, people-pleasing, putting others ahead of oneself. Client after client came through my doors, struggling with the feeling that they had given so much of themselves to others that there was nothing left. The struggle was very real for them … and real for me. I was doing everything to make other people happy yet was overwhelmed by unhappiness and emptiness on the inside.

Patterns of Giving and Guilt

Those of us who give too much of ourselves often do so because of a deeply internalized sense of guilt. We try to tell ourselves that our giving is an act of love—we repeat it like a mantra or a chant, over and over again, to make ourselves believe it. Clients come into my office, where they continue to repeat it. *I do it because I love them, because that's what a good parent, partner, employer, friend does.* But then my clients ask, *Why do I still feel so bad? Why do I feel like I can never give enough?*

This was the experience for one client, whom I'll call Janet. Janet felt like she had the perfect life, or at least that's what she thought she was supposed to feel. Career, husband, kids, friends, beautiful home, financial security … what more could Janet ask for? She had it all. For Janet, coming into therapy was to explore why, with all her blessings, she still felt so unhappy, empty, and depleted.

Our journey together began with exploring areas of struggle. Janet needed to become aware of similar patterns in her life as a child and as an adult, acknowledge how she learned to keep herself safe, and recognize her perceptions and expectations before she could connect to her deeper yearnings for fulfillment and how she wanted to experience her Self. This process of working together is rooted in the foundation of Satir Transformational Systemic Therapy, a modality that guides my practice. Janet became aware that she had adopted a pattern of taking care of everyone else in her life, ensuring their happiness and fulfillment. Janet assumed the role of being responsible "for" her husband's happiness, uplifting him, supporting him through his struggles socially and professionally, encouraging him, fulfilling all his emotional needs, and being there for him when he needed her. Janet swore that her husband did appreciate everything she did for him, their children, and their home. She was simply doing what a good wife, a good mother, a good loving person does. At least, that's what Janet had learned as a child and what she was now role modelling for her children. The message was: treat people the way you want to be treated even if they are hurtful and cruel to you. Smile, turn the other cheek, be the better person, give them more kindness. All the while, Janet coped by taking on a persona of placating, pleasing, and sacrificing. Implications that she was not following the rules would riddle her with guilt. Whatever Janet did, she was sure to not ruffle feathers, create conflict, or hurt someone's feelings. Hurting someone's feelings or causing disappointment was the worst thing she could do.

Janet's experiences are echoed by those of another of my clients, Trevor. Trevor learned at a very young age that in order to feel loved, appreciated, and worthy, he "needed to be" what others needed him to be. Like a chameleon scurrying around and changing its skin to accommodate, fit in, and hide from harm, Trevor mastered fulfilling other people's needs so that he wouldn't disappoint them. As Trevor moved into adulthood, he learned how to be the biggest and boldest knight, proudly taking on whatever obstacles came his way, including other people's challenges. Trevor earned himself a highly reputable position in his community and owned a very successful business where he was responsible for numerous staff. He became the person that people could count on: loving, committed, dedicated, passionate, loyal, fun, and determined. Trevor's self-appointed "saviour" role was fulfilling, and yet he experienced heaviness and loneliness. He noticed that his care and compassion for others started to take on a new form of anger and resentment. *Why is it that I do all this stuff for everyone else and make sure they are all taken care of, but nobody reaches out to me to see how I'm doing or appreciates me?* Was the question spiraling through Trevor's mind. Like Janet, Trevor was so determined to "be" the "perfect" person for everyone else that he gradually disconnected from who he was. What neither Trevor nor Janet realized was that their hard work in pleasing others was actually their way of striving for self-love. At the same time, it was destroying them. It was also destroying me.

Guilt had a strong hold on me from a very young age. My decisions in life, about how to respond to people and/or circumstances and how I showed up in the world, were literally based on fulfilling other people's expectations and perceptions. Like Janet, questions about the needs of others dominated my mind. *What would they think? What do they want me to say or do? Is this what will make them happy? How does this reflect on being a "good girl"?* Through the various developmental stages of life, adhering to the rules and expectations of family, religious beliefs, familial values, teachers, role models, and friends was paramount to my survival. Not meeting the explicit and implicit expectations felt like I was betraying or hurting others. When I reflect back on my experiences with guilt, I understand how the little prickly "squeezes" built up to have lasting impacts on my relationship with my Self, others, and the world. Unconsciously I became a servant to guilt, not having a voice or presence. The power of this little, aloof, displeased pink dragon called guilt continued to grow and in some areas of my life manifested into a large, red, standing, fierce, fire-breathing demon called shame. Shame taught me confusion, fear, hatred, betrayal, heaviness, and disconnection.

The only way I knew how to survive the pain of worthlessness and rejection was to give in to guilt by holding others' value and pleasure above my own. People-pleasing, placating, appeasing, self-deprecation, surviving, keeping peace, winning over, and self-abandonment are some of the names for the process I was loyal to.

As an adult, this familiar pattern became increasingly conscious and is known to me as torture in hell. Talking with Trevor, I resonated with his profound awareness so deeply that it hit the centre of my core. I too would invest so much of my time and energy taking care of everyone else's pain and suffering that there was no room for me. At times, my own Light and Love was either put aside or sacrificed completely. Like many clients who came into my life around this time, I would connect with others by putting myself in their shoes. This is called being empathetic. It means that to understand other people's experiences, I must put myself into their experiences. But here's the truth and blessing: their experiences are *not* my experiences to own; therefore, they are *not* my truth. I was not only taking care of their pain, I was owning their experiences.

We Should Just *Know*, Shouldn't We?

As people-pleasers, placaters, and carriers of others' pain, we often think that we should be able to predict our own needs just as well as we have trained ourselves to predict the needs of others. The hard truth is that years of shame and guilt, of hyper-focusing on other people, can block us from knowing where to start on our healing journeys. Sometimes we have become so distant from our Selves that we cannot even name the pain that we feel.

Janet knew what she was "supposed to" feel. She *should*, she insisted, feel so grateful and blessed for where she was and all that she had, especially since her previous marriage didn't end very well. But, for years Janet had felt sad in her marriage. She questioned her husband's faithfulness and was overwhelmed by all the responsibilities that came with being the best wife. But, how could she admit that? It would mean that she was struggling, that she was incompetent, selfish, weak, or, even worse, ungrateful. While she was acutely made aware by her husband that she should be grateful as he provided financial security for their family, Janet continued to struggle with the internal conflict of possibly not prioritizing her family or remaining in the marriage. A marriage that was one-sided and dominated by her husband. What about Janet's needs and aspirations? Doubt and insecurity reigned over her Soul. It was completely impossible for her to confidently make decisions on her own or ask for anything for herself.

Through all of this, Janet lost her zest for life—there was no joy and life became simply a task to accomplish. Her guilt kept her from questioning how her life was actually playing out. The change became so unconscious and gradual that she really believed and accepted that this was how life was supposed to be—take care of your husband and children, keep the peace, put on a smiling face, persevere through challenges, and present happiness. And, she was "supposed to" do all of this while being subjected to dismissive, condescending comments and being yelled at. How Janet's husband was treating her was emotional, psychological, and verbal abuse; however, she would never and could never admit that. What would that say about her? Justifications and excuses for his actions became constant: "He's stressed and overwhelmed with working so hard to take care of our family and all our needs. If it wasn't for how hard he works we wouldn't have all the things that we are blessed to have." This is the narrative that Janet convinced herself was her Truth.

In times of pain, and even in times of happiness, constructing narratives for ourselves is a coping mechanism. At the best of times, narratives help us reprocess our experiences from a safe distance, so we can reflect on how our realities have changed, how we have grown. But at other times, we have to tell ourselves stories to simply make it through the day, because facing reality would immobilize us. The issue is that after a while, we might become so convinced by our own stories that we can no longer see the things we've left out. Even if those things are our very Selves.

One day when I was working with Trevor, he was forced to confront his self-abandonment. As we spoke about his life, Trevor acknowledged all of his positive intentions and resources for changing his life. He began to realize that he had gathered all the people in his life into a warm and safe circle of support, appreciation, and love. Experiencing the feelings that manifested from honouring the compassionate space of love, Trevor connected to deep sadness when I asked him, "Where is Trevor in this circle of comfort?" It was at this moment that Trevor realized he did not think about or even include himself in the circle. I will always remember that day when Trevor became consciously aware that his actions of valuing others ahead of his Self was actually preventing him from deep fulfillment. As I experienced Trevor feeling safe in vulnerability and embracing courage, I witnessed him collapse his upper body over his knees. In this position, he then cradled his head in both of his hands and began weeping profusely. In silence, and with love and tenderness, Trevor connected to his deep emotions, allowing the years of hiding to have a voice. I'm giggling to myself as I write this now, recalling Trevor's heartfelt yet humorous announcement: he raised his head up, looked me straight in the eyes, and said, "So I just have to love myself? Well how the fuck do I do that?" This ignited Trevor's beautiful journey of rediscovering who he is, what he wants, and how to love himself.

As I saw this change in Trevor, I started to wonder about myself. *What do I want? How do I love myself? Who* am *I?* Like many people, I learned at a very young age how to keep myself safe. Yet, protecting myself was the very thing that kept me from being authentically me. I wanted to be true to my Self: as a therapist, I knew that I "should" be able to do the very thing I was counselling my clients to do. But, like a child yearning for comfort in the warmth of safety, fear flooded the desire and shifted to ego, judgments, and insecurities. Choosing me meant coming out from hiding and doing the hard, uncomfortable things. I envisioned: I could stay on the beach in certainty, watching the beauty of the waves, or I could get into the water, learn the movement, and be connected to the experience. I knew in my cognitive brain it was easier said than done, and my heart said it was way too scary to navigate the strong waves. That's it! I wanted to ride the waves without learning how to navigate the waters. *I know what it takes; I can offer the space, love, and support for others to do the hard, scary stuff, but no, not me ... I don't do the actual work to learn how to do it; I should just "know" how to do it and then do it.*

Doing the Hard Work

In our own ways, Janet, Trevor, and I had reached the point of complete depletion. We were struggling to make it through each day. Our stories were not going to change if we didn't make the changes. For me, leaving an unhealthy marriage, owning my voice, asserting boundaries, and standing in my Truth were some of the behavioural changes that were required to connect to Self love. These were not easy decisions, and they definitely came with some pain and struggle. It was the same for Janet and Trevor. Deepening our connections to Self required us to look at our fears, judgments, and insecurities, and expose ourselves to vulnerability, forgiveness, and love.

Moving into Self love is a journey that requires time, patience, compassion, and action. Literally dying inside, Janet knew that if things didn't change, she would not survive anymore but would succumb to a place of suffering. She knew she had to take action.

During our journey together, Janet systematically explored and processed both the negative and positive impacts of "keeping the peace." We did this by using expressive forms of therapy such as sand trays, guided visual meditations, conversations of curiosity, and connecting to her somatic experiences. Janet became consciously aware that the changes needed to come from a deep place within her Soul. She needed and wanted to experience her Self in a place of radiant light, full of love and vibrant life energy. For Janet, this meant changing her narrative of how she identified with her Self and doing something extremely foreign: valuing her Self. Janet discovered that if she was going to thrive, she needed to step into her own Truth. Stepping into her Truth meant connecting to her feelings and experiences and putting an end to the cycle of placating to guilt. Guilt had so much power over Janet that it had trapped her in a life of serving others. What appeared to be a quick decision in a lifelong battle, Janet connected to her determination and loyalty by proclaiming: "Enough is enough! I cannot and will not continue to suffer." This decision was birthed from a place of love … a deep love for her Self.

For Janet, loving her Self wasn't about standing up to her husband; rather, it was credited to honouring her Self and offering compassion to the terrified, lonely parts deep inside her which were flooded with guilt. Choosing to no longer hide behind fear, Janet stepped into love and chose peace, freedom, and harmony. This unexpected change did create some unsettling backlash for Janet as she worked through the blame, recurring messages of shame, expectations of acceptance and forgiveness, and accusations of infidelity. Ironically, Janet's husband was the one who had been having an affair for the previous nine years. The pain of her marriage ending and disappointing her family transformed into a precious gift of self-compassion and love: the choice of choosing her SELF. Janet and I celebrated the outcomes of her making the decision that was best for her as she also experienced positive changes in her relationships with her children.

Like Janet, Trevor made the choice to choose his Self with compassion, not empathy. Trevor learned that if he was going to survive, he needed to take care of himself and attend to his own wellness so he could authentically show up for those he cared about. When Trevor stepped into his Truth—which until then had been saturated in others' experiences and pain—the tears of relief emerged, flowing with this new awareness that he had the choice to make decisions around what's best for him. This is truly the only control that he gets to have. Trevor had been choosing others over himself. By protecting others from their pain, he was not allowing those individuals in his life to experience vulnerability and the human struggles that are presented along the journey of life.

This hit me hard! There's my Truth: I wanted to protect my children and take care of their pain so badly that I became consumed with their and many others' struggles so that I didn't need to explore my own pain…. I was adamantly avoiding vulnerability. Witnessing Trevor, Janet, and so many other clients move from being guarded with ego and protection into a place of surrendering in the glorious, difficult place of vulnerability was inspiring … it was intimate. The grace of releasing control (the need to be perfect and certain) allows us to invite in and receive serenity and peace. But, this can only begin to happen in a space of safety. It happened in that one profound session when I observed Trevor experiencing an intimate connection with his Self. Energetically and intentionally holding the space for Trevor to *be* in deep Self love and tenderness was sacred and honouring. If there was ever a time to experience "the gift of tears," it was in that moment. Trevor's gift of Self love ignited the beginning of my own journey of manifesting love and compassion for myself. Trevor returned for a few sessions to strengthen and root into his new foundation of being authentic without guilt. This process was challenging and hard, courageous, scary, painful, and joyful, all at the same time. It brought many tears of hurt and sadness in unravelling the impacts of his past, but also tears of joy that sprang from new awarenesses and decisions.

The transformations within my clients were noticeable as their energy, physical appearances, and verbal expressions changed. I also wanted to experience this change. To feel the burden and heaviness turn into light and freedom. To connect with my Self from a place of appreciation, honour, and love. To release the past in order to receive the present and welcome excitement for the future.

Trevor's experiences in particular showed me the gift of being vulnerable and doing the hard work. Doing the hard stuff meant being vulnerable, exposed ... naked to the truth, facing the dragons and demons of hell. It felt like torture, to be honest. Doing the hard work was truly about being vulnerable with my Self and going to those scary places that were so deeply hidden. A significant dark place that I needed to navigate through was the belief, and the reality, that saying "yes" to Me could make others uncomfortable or even emotionally hurt them. Realizing I could possibly hurt someone emotionally was paralyzing as this experience was extremely familiar to me. I had endured emotional abuse from childhood to adult-hood, and it had become so painful that guilt surfaced to protect the anguish of the Truth. At the time, it seemed far better to blame myself than blame others. But this only locked in all the pain. I knew I would have to allow the pain to be real: acknowledge it and offer it compassion and understanding. I could not just sit in the suffering of the pain and say "This is painful." I had to say, "Yes, this exists, and now what can I do to change this?" I needed to go through my own pain—feel the pain in order to heal the pain.

I do not believe "time heals." Rather, time conceals—it's the act of Self love that heals. But I wondered ... *Am I important enough and deserving of breaking free from the chains of guilt? Do I also get to have peace and harmony in my life?* "Yes" was the only response in my soul as I connected to love, compassion, and faith. Appreciating the experiences of Janet, Trevor, and so many other beautiful people whom I've had the honour to work with, I decided I "get" to have love and joy in my soul. I embraced the idea that happiness is a birthright. Focusing on my deep yearnings for value, respect, and purpose, I began my own path of healing. This journey—which is really never-ending until the day I die—involved my own deep personal work. I did the vulnerable work in counselling (with multiple counsellors, I might add), reflected on and connected to the experiences of my clients, and truly did the things I asked my clients to do: the hard stuff ("practice what you preach," right?). I also listened to incredibly insightful podcasts and learned how to *be* with my Self. I made the decision to choose me, and with this decision my energy changed.

For so much of my life, I had learned to be extremely busy, always doing for others, taking care of them, and being extremely purposeful and achieving great things so that I could avoid failure and be accepted and valued by others, which is what I so desperately wanted. My healing embraced slowing down. I realized that I needed to be more intentional about myself and about how I pay attention to my own experiences, reactions, thoughts, feelings, and perceptions of myself and others. I had to sit in silence, listening to my Truth, not my fears. This was difficult for me. I did not want to face the reality of my Truth—the truth that there was a possibility that if I choose me, I may be hurting others; others may not accept me or may even reject me. The challenge with facing guilt head-on is the backlash of judgment, the voices that tell you, *You need to hold on and think about others; you should be saving your marriage; stay committed to your family; if family's so important to you, you can't neglect or turn your back on your family; you're a counsellor, you should know....* These chaotic but powerful thoughts flooded my mind like fierce waves crashing over me, knocking me off balance. But I wanted to persevere. I wanted to choose me.

Facing my pain and surrendering to guilt allowed for me to be open and honest with my Self. This vulnerable space allowed for me to choose me. When I created the space to be with my Self, I found it healing and profound to write my pain a letter. Offering validity, honour, and compassion to my pain provided closure to the suffering and created an opening for healing. I then got to write a letter to my Self extending forgiveness and love. The journey of healing continued for me by sharing my tenderness with others. This was also very scary. It activated a lot of old beliefs and judgments. And I discovered that I couldn't be wide open with anyone and everyone. (I did this and experienced the hurtful impacts.) Presenting my authentic Self required me to feel safe. I mean, who wants to go into those scary places and feel unsafe? I, like many clients, needed to feel safe in order to connect with my tenderness. Exposing my raw naked Truth was terrifying in the beginning, but with supportive individuals in my life, I soon felt cocooned in love and safety. This comfort offered me the opportunity to be vulnerable and be authentically me.

Through all of this, I also grew as a therapist. My work as a therapist evolved from being a container of my clients' sad stories to creating a sacred place where clients can be seen in their pain. In this sacred place, people can connect to themselves so that they can become empowered to make whatever decision is best for them. There is no way I can fully understand other people's experience; however, I can learn what it's like for them and how their experiences have impacted them. I can listen, validate, reflect back, hold space, and "see them" in *their* struggle. This is compassion. Compassion offers love to others and love to Self without guilt or judgment. It's a softening of ease and a welcoming of acceptance of what is. By allowing others to *own* their stories, positive and negative, I am allowing them to experience empowerment, connect to their voice, and have a sense of agency. This process is choosing Self … it's Self love. From this place of love, I can choose what's best for me. Harnessing my love protects me from the continuation of a generational entrapment of guilt.

Seeing my clients' breakthroughs impacted me at my deep spiritual core, a place of affirmation, a "knowing." This place resides in the calm, peaceful retreating of the waves back into the ocean. Accepting I am human and opening up to receiving all of me, I choose me and I now show up in relationships as being authentically me. With this comes the acceptance that there will be people in my life who no longer like, want, or accept this version of me.

My journey with clients is not about telling them they must disconnect from negative people in their lives. Rather, I try to bring into their awareness that this might be what happens. Supporting individuals with love and acceptance also means preparing them to face the reality that they may lose some people in their life and that they need to be okay with that. As I became more aware of this myself, I could freely and consciously make the compassionate choice to choose me, and it's more than okay that I left my marriage, it's more than okay to not chase unfilled relationships, it's okay if other people make the choice to blame or reject me, I'm okay … I'm more than okay because I am honouring and loving me in my authentic Self.

Healing the Generational Guilt

The most noticeable and rewarding changes from doing the hard, uncomfortable work are in my relationships with my two beautiful children. The impact of my personal growth is that I have more patience with them and the desire and energy to be actively involved in their lives. I can be intentionally present and attuned to their experiences, responding to them with calmness and understanding while also asserting boundaries with confidence. I can offer so much love. Parenting without guilt freed me from this need to be "perfect," and I could begin to role model to my children the act of being human.

At first, this new version of me appeared to be unsettling for my daughter Samantha. I imagine her experience was that of confusion—"Who is this woman saying 'no' to me?" I also experienced Samantha not feeling very safe with the disruption of her reality of what constituted "family" and how she possibly perceived me. Overwhelmed with fear and guilt through my new transition, my motherly gifts were less than impeccable and not that of honour as I started to project anger and sadness. However, as I continued my path of healing and began to integrate choices that honour me, I noticed Samantha learning resilience, honour, and how to protect her Self with boundaries of Self love. I could see her owning her voice. I've been blessed with developing and co-creating a deep and meaningful relationship with my daughter that supports all her emotions and struggles. Life at times is not easy; it can actually be extremely painful, but with "Mamma Bear" holding space for acceptance, honour, and love, my daughter is safe to be her Self and make decisions that she feels/believes are best for her. Oh, don't get me wrong—Mamma Bear still needs to come out at times, but it's by knowing what my daughter needs in those moments that I can allow her to learn and navigate her own journey. Samantha experiences the impacts of her decisions, and she learns and grows from the choices she makes. What I am most proud of is that she is learning how to establish boundaries with people around her, she is speaking her Truth, and most importantly she is releasing the generational claws of guilt.

From my perception, the impacts of my decision to choose Me were definitely experienced differently by each child. For a long time, my son struggled to process and express his emotions. As a toddler and young child, Brady would experience explosive reactions to things, resulting in verbal, emotional, and at times physical outbursts. This pattern went on for years as I so desperately attempted to offer his anger love and compassion. Nothing seemed to distract, redirect, change, or transform his emotional struggles, until I chose to do something differently. The beautiful gift of reciprocity is the lovely flow of giving and receiving. When I offered Brady a confident, stable, compassionate, strong, and loving mom, I received a soft, tender, caring, and loving son in return. This is *who* my son is and continues to be with me as he learns to navigate life's challenges. Standing up to guilt permitted me to show my son that struggling is real and it's okay to be vulnerable—it's safe to be vulnerable. This feels so incredibly hard for him, and I honour Brady in *all* of who he is. Guilt is hard, overwhelming, consuming, and scary, like the powerful crashing waves, while love is soft, peaceful, free, and serene, like the tide retreating back into the calm ocean. Life is about both, and both of my children get to experience a loving mom to help guide them in their own journeys.

Witnessing Janet's compassionate Self love and Trevor's courageous vulnerability opened my consciousness to having this harmony in my own personal life. I learned from their exemplary experiences and deeply connected to their empowering choices. I understood that this empowerment requires us to move from a cognitive understanding of the importance of Self and spiritual care to actually embodying the action of choosing one's Self. I wanted this level of compassion for my Self, and I was inspired to change. Moving through chaos and vulnerability allowed me to show up in my Truth and give voice to my own experiences, resulting in freedom. Closing the door on guilt also permitted a deeper and more present version of my Self with my own children.

Being aware of the source of our struggles is the first step to healing. It is then our responsibility to decide what we want to do with that awareness. My personal reflection and awareness is that while I was holding space to support (and sometimes owning) the healing of other people's pain, I was not doing this very act of love for myself. I needed and wanted what my clients learned in our sessions together, which was that the boundaries of Self love and honour = reciprocity = a Beautiful Infinite Gift!

About Corrinna Douglas

Corrinna Douglas, MA, RCC, is very passionate about supporting people's growth and empowerment. With over twenty years of experience working with children, adolescents, at-risk youth, families, and vulnerable populations, Corrinna connects with individuals by offering a space for authenticity, safety, and honour. By helping individuals navigate through life experiences and reconnecting them with their inner strengths and resources, Corrinna shows them how healing and change is possible. Her compassionate, supportive, and collaborative approach offers a deeper and meaningful journey of discovery. Through discovery, exploration, and curiosity, Corrinna guides individuals toward becoming more aware of their truth and to connect to it so that they may make the best life decisions for themselves. This process can offer deep and lasting change in their lives. Corrinna holds a Bachelor of Criminal Justice and a Master of Clinical Counselling Psychology. She is also a Registered Clinical Counsellor with the British Columbia Association of Clinical Counsellors and a clinical member of the Satir Institute of the Pacific.

www.CorDiscovery.ca
corrinna@cordiscovery.ca
www.facebook.com/cordiscovery.counselling/

3

Intergenerational Healing

By Lyla Harman

*If intergenerational trauma can alter DNA,
why can't intergenerational love?*

— **Alicia Elliott**

Intergenerational Healing

By Lyla Harman

What I hear from my ancestors is … Listen to the water, listen to the sky—let the wind kiss your ears and tell you their story.… You are blessed, as are all Creator's beings. You have truth and love in your heart to give, and you don't need doubt to get in your way. There *is* a healing path. Lhexunt thunu sheshlh siem. Lhexunt thunu thele' 'i' suli. Lhexunt thunu sts'lhhwulmuhw. *Bless my path Creator. Bless my heart and spirit. Bless my First Nations people.* Let the voices of our ancestors come forward. You are chosen for we could not and now we can through you. Be humble, be kind, know your truth. Let it be told as it is without prejudice, judgment, or blame. Be the change you wish to see in our community—no cliché, only truth. Let the tears drop to Mother Earth and be healed as only She knows how …

I hear this truth that it's okay to share my story, and yet there is this overwhelming internal pressure to shut up and be quiet. *Who am I to complain? Who am I to clam the impact of intergenerational trauma?*

This dialogue swings in my head like a pendulum between accepting *all* of me and dismissing my story and lived experience. This experience is echoed in the stories of every single one of my community members. To be pounded by pain and then judge ourselves for complaining. Every single Indigenous woman I know feels the reality of compound trauma. It is just another day in the life of Indigenous women, impacted by addictions, sexual abuse, the Indian Residential School system, the Sixties Scoop, the patriarchy of the Indian Act, colonization, racism, and domestic violence. Not one trauma but many traumas endlessly interweaving, making their impact all the worse as they amplify each other.

How do we heal from this? How do we role model for our children what we have never seen ourselves? How do we retell our narrative? Our Elders say that healing comes from knowing who we are and where we come from. So let's start there … I am of Quw'utsun, Secwépemc, English, and Scottish decent. My mom had me at fifteen years old, straight out of Indian Residential School, where "The nuns never taught me sex education," she said. She was bold enough to tell the social workers who came to claim me the day I was born to "Get the fuck out! This is my baby!" I didn't know I had a birth father until I was eighteen years old—he had walked out before I was born. That is the reason my mom gave me her maiden name—she was going to raise me herself.

My mom was my warrior—she is the strongest woman I know. I attribute my greatest teachings to her. So, why haven't we talked in six years?

My theory of why my mother and I have not spoken in six years is tied to compound trauma and intergenerational abandonment. My hope is to explore intergenerational abandonment and how it impacts my family and my work in Indigenous communities so we can create a healing path. We can only see where we are going by understanding where we have come from. When we see the devastation of colonization, a path becomes clear. We can move from patterns of hurt and pain by shedding personal shame and blame. Then we can make new choices and be our authentic selves.

So, what is intergenerational abandonment? Intergenerational abandonment is part of the intergenerational trauma inflicted on Indigenous people by European and Canadian colonizers, especially through the Indian Residential School system. For over 120 years, Indigenous parents were forced by the Canadian government to send their children, some as young as two years old, to prison-like schools. The purpose of these schools was to assimilate Indigenous people into mainstream society. *Once there, the children were abused—physically, mentally, emotionally, spiritually, and sexually—and, with the discovery of thousands of mass graves, sometimes murdered by the priests, nuns, and teachers who ran the schools.* If parents refused to send their children, they were thrown into prison. The devastation wrought by the Indian Residential School system is profound. There, generations of children turned into adult survivors who lost their Indigenous language, culture, identity, and sense of belonging.

As humans, we know what we know and act how we act because of our DNA and how we were raised. Our life experiences can become encoded in our DNA and passed on to our children. In this way, when unchecked, traumatic pain patterns get passed down from generation to generation. Intergenerational abandonment, in my experience and observation, occurs because of complex post-traumatic stress inflicted in person and through DNA. For Indigenous people, the abandonment experienced by generations of children in the Indian Residential School system has been personalized onto parent and self, so that it feels like the pain and trauma were caused not by the government or the teachers but by your parent and self. This can result in many ways of coping such as depression, shame, self-blame, a fear of abandonment, low self-esteem, addictions, and suicide.

In my family, my mom stated she felt abandoned by her mom for sending her to the Indian Residential School. For this reason, my mom was distant with her mom and close to her dad. My experience with my grandmother was different. I was the oldest granddaughter and Grandma took care of me when my mom went back to school. We were close—Grandma loved me unconditionally.

These patterns play out in my current relationship with my mom and children. My son is close to my mom. He blames me for being distant with her and told me that he's doing the same to me. So many families I've worked with have this same pattern of abandonment or disconnection between family members. We try so hard to break the cycle of pain only to be tumbled in the waves of it. Even when I can see the wave coming and prepare for it, I'm swept up in its power, tumbled, and spit out, riddled with sand and grit.

And yet, even amidst the pain, something inside me says I'm to be grateful, and I am! I am blessed! I have a supportive, loving husband and two beautiful children. I love the work I do as a mental health counsellor in my Indigenous community. It is my calling, my purpose. It gives me meaning.

So, how do we resist the intergenerational pull? How do we stop the patterns of pain? I believe that if the Indigenous people impacted by generations of Indian Residential Schools can understand the system of colonization, they can free themselves from the burden of personal shame, begin the decolonization process, and open opportunities for healing.

* * *

In my work as a mental health therapist in a Coast Salish community, we never used the term "clients"—we used community members. This is a purposeful, non-hierarchical approach to signify that I am a community member on my healing journey kwun'atsustul, *walking hand in hand*, with community members on their healing journey. Quite the opposite concept of the typical "doctor-patient" relationship.

Althea, one of my resilient community members, came to counselling to work through the abandonment she experienced from her mother and her daughter, and therefore her two-year-old granddaughter. She realized that her maternal family line had experienced four generations of abandonment. Her mom was raised by her grandmother as a cultural expectation. Often in our Coast Salish communities, the eldest grandchild was traditionally raised by their grandparents. Althea herself was raised by multiple aunties, uncles, and grandparents, as her parents were unable to be there in her early childhood years.

I first met Althea over fifteen years ago as a young mom in the Butterfly Women program, a women's program for healing from childhood sexual abuse. Even back then I could see her bright light shine. She was involved in our Coast Salish paddling, culture, and traditions. She was eager to face all her fears!

Living in small, intimate Indigenous communities can be like living in a fishbowl. When Althea was going through her divorce, she faced a harsh, judgmental atmosphere—everyone had an opinion and fingers to point. Althea did what she thought was right: to keep her children in their home community and not uproot them in the divorce. So, she left the community, and the children stayed with their father. Unfortunately, her daughter saw this as abandonment—a valid and common reaction in our Indigenous communities still dealing with the devastation of Indian Residential School.

So how was I able to help Althea, and she in turn help me? The healing process in action …

Althea and I had years of on-off work together to establish a foundation of safety and trust built on a wholistic approach of balancing her physical, mental, emotional, and spiritual healing. As I use a trauma-informed approach in therapy, Althea had choice and voice in her healing plan. We agreed to do EMDR—Eye Movement Desensitization and Reprocessing.[1] During an EMDR session, eye movements or bilateral taps are combined with guided instructions that help community members access memories of traumatic events. Using eye movements in a guided way allows people to reprocess what they remember from the negative event. Special attention is paid to negative self-image/belief, emotion, and bodily sensations related to the given event. By reprocessing the event in this way, EMDR can "repair" or heal the injury from that memory and aid the community member in moving to a positive belief/self-image which would indicate that the issue is resolved.

EMDR is one of the therapeutic tools, second to the Satir Model, I find most helpful in the healing in Indigenous communities. While EMDR is typically useful for working to resolve a single episode traumatic event, Althea and I agreed to use it because we had a strong foundation of internal resource development to prepare her to work through potential triggers. We agreed to do an EMDR exercise on the "abandonment" between herself and her daughter.

During the EMDR floatback exercise, Althea did taps and connected to: a negative image—a four-year-old girl in a room alone, unkempt in a red dress; the belief—"I'm damaged, ugly, and not smart enough"; the emotion—scared and alone; and the bodily sen-

---

1   To learn more about EMDR, visit the website for the EMDR Institute: https://www.emdr.com/what-is-emdr/

sation—fear in her chest.

This image was Althea's four-year-old self. As she was able to have a safe distance and see things from her adult perspective, she was able to see not only the four-year-old girl, she was also able to see her parents in the far background, caught in their own traumas. Because she could see the ways that trauma limited her parents' ability to take care of her, she no longer needed to shame and blame herself for feeling damaged, ugly, and not smart enough. Furthermore, she no longer had to shame and blame her parents. She understood that their trauma was the cause of the abandonment—her parents' trauma in action.

Once Althea made this connection, she was able to nurture her inner child by picturing her adult-self giving compassionate care and understanding to her inner four-year-old child. I encouraged Althea's adult-self to allow her inner child to "grow-up"—to picture nurturing herself developmentally at ten years old, fifteen, twenty, thirty, until she was her current age. At each age, Althea was able to give precisely what her inner child needed for safety, trust, and love. Virginia Satir believed this exercise imperative to ensuring that we, as adults, can connect with all our fully developed inner resources and not leave parts of ourselves underdeveloped.

Althea ended the session with the positive belief "I am strong and resilient," stating that she had brand new eyes, a weight was lifted, and she could feel relief in her chest. It wasn't until months later that Althea shared with me her breakthrough with her daughter.

* * *

Althea told me if I don't tell my story then it's a breeding ground for blame, misunderstanding, alienation, and doubt. For so long, I didn't tell my children my story because I thought I wanted to protect them from getting caught in the crossfire of family dynamics or the pressure of having to take sides. So, I protected them, and still ended up recreating the alienation that I feared. Creator help me!

On the outside, my family was the perfect nuclear family: a hard-working logging father and a stay-at-home mom with a daughter and son. We would hunt, fish, camp, visit family, live with family, or have family live with us. My younger brother and I lived with our parents, grandparents, and great grandparents, farming and living off the land. We understood the value of hard work. But, at times, on the inside, my family seemed like a nuclear bomb that had exploded. I lived in twenty-two houses by the time I was eighteen, experienced sexual abuse from three of my closest family members, and witnessed familial domestic violence, extreme alcoholism, and the constant infidelity of my dad.

Through it all, my mom was the greatest cheerleader in my life. She was positive and openly expressed her love with hugs. She made birthdays and holidays special, and she was fearlessly protective—I remember her calling out my fifth-grade teacher for not putting me in for a volleyball game. She was supportive and relentlessly creative with resources: sewing, cooking, canning—you name it, she could do it. She believed me when I was ten years old and disclosed that I was sexually abused, and as a young mom of twenty-five years old, she took my brother and I to safety. She role modelled how to go after what you want without letting anything get in your way. She filled me with absolute unconditional love! Hmm, there are those words again—unconditional love …

So how did we go from best friends to not talking? For me, she began to change when I started creating my own small family. It was then that she became unfiltered, mean, and hurtful. She has no recognition of the impact her words have on others. When anyone dares to call her out on her behaviour, she simply responds, "That's me and if you don't like it—fuck off!" People fear her. Her anger, negativity, and unwillingness to keep any of it in check pushes people away. In our Indigenous community, we call this lateral violence— when our people pick up hurt and pain from colonization and begin to hurt each other.

I tried everything to make our relationship work—to listen, to not take her hurt to heart, to encourage her, to focus on the positive, to not change her, to say to my kids, "We don't talk that way or treat people that way—that's just Grandma." I took courses on non-violent communication, thinking that would give me more skills to deal with her anger and sharp tongue. But none of it was enough.

The damage was severe. I felt abandoned by my mom. My mental and emotional state was being taken over, consumed by feeling Not Good Enough. After each visit with my mom, I felt like a mountain lion had clawed open my chest, leaving my heart exposed and oozing. Because it's never a parent's fault, the child always blames themself. I would convince myself that if I acted better, I wouldn't get hurt. If I avoided the "landmine" topics, then I'd be safe. Only soon enough I realized that it didn't matter what topic I avoided—everything set her off. So, the visits got shorter and shorter. Even then I would leave having to remove multiple arrows from my strongest armour of acceptance, compassion, and understanding.

I spoke to a counsellor friend who said, "Lyla why do you take it? You need to set a healthy boundary. This relationship is not healthy; it's toxic and damaging you!" The hurt and pain got so big that I needed to stop all contact. But, you don't abandon your mom who has done absolutely everything for you. It's Mom—she was my *best friend*. It was only when it came to setting a boundary around my cubs that the mother bear came out in me and I said "NO" and walked away.

I've had years of therapy, and my husband has immense patience for listening to my feelings, thoughts, and grief over my mom. Yes, grief—I didn't know you could grieve someone who is alive, but I do. I know I could call her and go to her home to visit, yet the conversation would be with the shell of the person I once knew.

* * *

Any time I am stuck, I pray. Any time I am grateful, I pray. I am a spiritual person, and this is a far cry from being religious. I respect all people and their beliefs—except when those beliefs colonize and damage another.

I pray to Creator to guide me on this wound in my life.

And the answer that stands out so strong and continues to inspire me is the fierce unconditional love and family connection of our Indigenous women.

This is me trying to make sense of the chaos—to make meaning. To selectively take from my shattered heart and decipher a new stained-glass picture that my mind, heart, and soul can comprehend. If this is all intergenerational abandonment—what is intergenerational healing?

When I was invited to write this chapter on the reciprocity of therapy, my wise young Elder-in-training Althea came to me in prayer. Our stories of intergenerational abandonment and healing overlapped in many ways. I immediately called her to ask if I could include her healing journey in this chapter. She answered the video call with her two-year-old granddaughter in her arms, and said, "Look Lyla, we did it!" She had reconnected with her daughter and granddaughter!

With proud tears I asked, "How did you do it?"

She shared:

"It has to do with empathy and compassion. We all did the best we could, coping with our trauma. It took great acts of faith to put myself out there and text my daughter—'Hi my girl, checking on you and hoping you are well, have a good day.' Constantly putting myself out there. Even when she wouldn't respond, I kept trying. In the process of putting myself out there, I wanted to connect—I wanted my children to know I'm here, I'm waiting. It's about constantly being vulnerable. I needed to repair what was broken in the relationship with my kids after the divorce. I still text every day and they text me back. In the beginning it might have been only a few moments of time with them. But I kept showing up. It hurts to feel the rejection in the moment, but I keep doing it! It's literally happening in the moment. We have hiccups, and I'm always telling myself if she's distant or unresponsive, that she's just where she's at, and I have compassion for that. I create boundaries when I need to, and I am ready to give immediate forgiveness. It's hard— really hard at times. As a parent, I continue to love but from afar—we need to accept that because it's a reflection of where our children are at on their journeys. And then it's back to compassion—because our ego likes to judge."

Althea had wisdom to share on intergenerational trauma and healing too:

"I believe it's a battle of dark energy and light energy when we process our trauma. That's where the healing is, because you transmute the energy. Transmute the energy means shifting the energy of your universe from dark to light— dark is blame, victim mode, and isolation. To heal, you have

to change the energy within you to compassion, forgiveness, and understanding. Trauma lives in the dark energy, and that's how we pass it to each other. It's so hard for us as Indigenous people because we're talking about generations of this pain that we're trying to peel back—that's why we need intergenerational healing! When I struggle with my mom, I have to circle back to acceptance—I have to accept that is where Mom is at. She chooses to heal or not. She stays in her pattern. Accepting, understanding, and choosing to forgive—that's the recipe. It can be difficult, but I work on it all the time."

Then I did what therapists are *not* supposed to do: I vulnerably asked Althea about myself. "What do you think I need with my son and my mom?"

She shared:

"It boils down to you just taking a breath. You just got to relax. When you think about them, it heightens your nervous system, even if you say something different in your mind. Your nervous system is responding = take a breath. If you are loved from afar, accept that. Or, if you know you're ready, you can start reaching out. You can say 'I want you to know I love you' and see where it goes from there."

Althea was able to acknowledge the complexity of intergenerational abandonment. She was able to see the bigger picture and lift the personal guilt and shame and see that abandonment, as a result from colonization, has been passed through our collective Indigenous genetic imprinting. By accepting, connecting with, and nurturing her inner child, she gave herself space to see that her mother did not abandon her but did the best she could. Althea is doing the best she can with her daughter by truly listening and continuing to show up, being patient, and having acceptance. She continues to create a strong path of decolonizing herself by reconnecting to who she is and where she comes from, her Coast Salish culture, traditions, family, and community. She made space for a new relationship with four generations—her mother, daughter, granddaughter, and *herself*.

I sat with Althea's wise words, her vulnerable healing, and invited my own reflection and processing.

Creator—tth'ihwum lhexunt thunu shelh. *Please bless my path.* I shared with my son, "If I treated you harshly or if anyone does for that matter, you need to set healthy boundaries. Even with me." And this is where I need strength, Creator—guide and heal me because I don't believe I treat him harshly. I try to understand—try to be open and full-hearted to listen, really listen with my heart so I can understand, connect, and make space for healing. And yet my need to be heard gets in the way. As soon as I start defending, I shut all doors to connection. So how do I validate my son's experience of being distant with me and still be true to myself? How do I accept his narrative, which contradicts my own, and move forward? I'm absolutely sure this is what my mom feels—that my narrative is skewed and far from the truth, just as it was with her relationship with her mother.

I know my mom made every sacrifice for me and my brother growing up. As I have done for my son and daughter. So Creator, how do I move forward?

More wisdom from Althea:

> *"Another pattern is—our eldest children witnessed us in our trauma. So, we need much more patience and compassion for our older children because they witnessed our trauma before we started doing our healing work."*

Once again, Althea is right! I was still growing up myself when I was raising my son at twenty-five years old. Things were different when I had my daughter at thirty-four—I gained self-esteem, spirituality, and more patience. No wonder my son's experience of me is entirely different from my daughter's.

When I started this vulnerable journey and read my first draft of this chapter to our intuitive publisher Julie Ann, she asked me to contact my twenty-three-year-old son and my fifteen-year-old daughter and ask four questions: How do you see me as a mother? How do you feel about the relationship that I have with your grandma? What do you think I need in my relationship with you? What do you think I need in my relationship with Grandma?

This is what my insightful fifteen-year-old wrote back:

1. how i see you as a mother: i love how you always have your family's best interests at heart and how you put so much time into me and dad to make our family work. though you're a super busy person, you always have a great attitude when it comes to keeping a positive mindset and being able to give advice when it comes to my problems/worries. i love how you always think big on what you want to do and take little steps toward your big goals. i've been able to learn not to be so hard on myself and to be easygoing whether it's with friends or soccer.

2. how i feel about you and grandma's relationship: a year ago i blamed you for me not being able to see or talk to grandma and i didn't get it. i've never seen grandma as a person who deserved to be ignored by

her family. after getting an understanding of what trauma and growth you went through i found it easier to understand how you have your personal limits and boundaries you set. just because you aren't close and don't reach out to her doesn't mean you haven't tried before, and clearly it didn't work for you as you two changed.

3. what i think you should do in our relationship: being able to listen to me and make me feel heard is something you've changed and been able to do. (wouldn't change anythin.)

4. what i think you need to do with you and grandma's relationship: now knowing where you're coming from with the relationship feeling one-sided and toxic, i don't blame you for taking a break. i think being able to listen and hear how you view the situation would help her get a better understanding (or make her more upset not sure) but i think it would help you feel some kind of closure, whether you end up sorting it out or not. maybe reaching out to her would help you communicate with my brother? (though it doesn't seem like he has any reason to try to hurt you.)

Okay, so what I read is that: as a mom I have my family's best interest at heart, I have a great attitude and positive mindset, I think big and take little steps to reach my goals, I teach that you shouldn't be so hard on yourself, and that when my daughter understood my trauma and growth it made it easier for her to understand me. And maybe I need to reach out to my mom for closure.

Wow, reading this felt like a "lightbulb moment": the fact that I was finally ready to hear this made me feel that I could put it into motion.

I am humbled by such insight and wisdom—this is the truest evidence of intergenerational healing!

I took my daughter's advice and reached out to my mom, with no answer back. I accept that my mom and I will likely not resolve our differences. Not in this human life form. Today, when I grieve her, I wrap her in love and light. And what I believe on a soul level is that we love one another—that is solid truth! That this abandonment is a small blink in our soul life, and when we meet on the other side our hearts will speak the language of knowingness that our human minds cannot comprehend.

As for my son, he had the same four questions, and he stated he wanted more time to think on it. I respected him and that decision. He is a deep thinker and feeler! If I listen to anything I've learned from this healing process, it's that if I have great faith and compassion, and if I keep showing up and truly listen, then I can mend the tear inside me and the tear in my relationship with my son.

One month later, I phoned my son to circle around to those four questions and "keep showing up." He stated that he was overwhelmed, and there was a long silence.... I went into my head and began to over-analyze and build my defence. But then I told myself *No! Don't go down that old path.* I quickly went to my heart for a response and said gently, "How can we move forward?" Another long silence. I asked what he needs. He said, "To see you." We turned on video chat and started talking about everyday things. I took a big breath and shared ... "I guess you don't know why I walked away from Grandma, and I take responsibility for that. I'm guessing it was sudden and confusing. Do you want to hear some of my story?" He stated, "That would be helpful." I started to share: the complexity of why I created strong boundaries and that these decisions were made in deep, long reflection, from love … That I grieve … That I am trying to understand the pain patterns and to heal with dignity and respect … That this conversation is us creating a new strengthened relationship … And that most of all, we can overcome any obstacle when two people are willing. I shared this is the beginning of my story and told him there is much more. He listened, thanked me, and said we need to do more of this. My heart exploded to hear of a path to move forward!

When we continue on our healing journeys, we can shine a light on new possibilities for ourselves and others—that is the gift of reciprocity! Thank you, Althea! The issues in our Indigenous communities continue to be complex—there is no single answer to healing. Awareness and decolonization are unique in each Indigenous community. For myself, I am never alone in the work I do. I am strongly connected to my ancestors and Creator. I sense their guidance to decolonize myself to know who I am and where I come from. They inspire me to connect to spirit, prayer, culture, learn Hul'q'umi'num', sing traditional songs, follow cultural teachings, listen to Elders, and support others. I learn from colonization, grow from it, and heal from it. When I can do that, it heals my ancestors who may not have had these opportunities in their lifetime.

Listen to the water, listen to the sky—let the wind kiss your ears and tell you their story.… You are blessed as are all Creator's beings. You have truth and love in your heart to give, and you don't need doubt to get in your way. There *is* a healing path. Lhexunt thunu sheshlh siem. Lhexunt thunu thele' 'i' suli. Lhexunt thunu sts'lhhwulmuhw. *Bless my path Creator. Bless my heart and spirit. Bless my First Nations people.*

About Lyla Harman

As an Indigenous woman, Lyla Harman, MSW, RSW, values the connection and healing that occurs while working with other Indigenous women. Lyla is a Registered Social Worker with the BC College of Social Workers and supports Coast Salish communities healing from trauma. Her passion is using Satir Transformational Systemic Therapy as a trauma-informed approach. In January 2018, Lyla opened Cedar Wellness Counselling and Consulting, a private practice based on growth, wisdom, and new possibilities. She challenges herself to continue her own healing so she can share this with those she works with. Lyla lives on Vancouver Island and enjoys spending time in nature with her husband, daughter, and son. She continues to decolonize herself by learning her traditional Hul'q'umi'num' language, songs, and teachings from the Quw'utsun Elders.

www.cedarwellness.ca
www.facebook.com/lyla.harman.52/
www.linkedin.com/in/lyla-harman-2695a480/
lyla.harman@cedarwellness.ca

4

Reciprocity in the Transformation of Shame into Self-Love

by Nancy M. Gordon

If we can share our story with someone who responds with empathy and understanding, shame cannot survive.

— **Brené Brown**

Reciprocity in the Transformation of Shame into Self-Love

by Nancy M. Gordon

We all have moments like this. When something happens that dramatically affects our life, sometimes even changing our whole life course. Life-defining moments can be positive in nature, like graduating from high school or getting married, or they can be profoundly life-changing in ways that seem devastating, like being injured in a car accident or losing a loved one. How we *perceive* these life-defining moments makes all the difference in how we experience and respond to them.

Life-defining moments often require us to make choices that we wouldn't otherwise have had to make about who we are, how we function, or how we live. But most important of all, life-defining moments open a pathway to choose *who we become as a result of those moments.*

I am a Licensed Clinical Social Worker, and for many years I enjoyed a thriving practice in which I worked with clients who had low self-esteem and who were dealing with childhood traumas. Along with low self-esteem, many of my clients felt extreme shame and loss throughout their lives. I, on the other hand, had high self-esteem and believed I was fulfilling my life's purpose by helping others. I felt I was living a life of "Divine Greatness" in which the most authentic parts of me were integrally connected to Spirit and therefore to my highest self. Yet, I was also a perfectionist. I held high standards for myself which, in hindsight, also led me to experience a sense of shame whenever a metaphorical flashlight illuminated some imperfections. Still, I felt successful and that I was walking the life path I was intended to. Until I was in a devastating car accident. In an instant, when the metal of our two cars collided, my path was forever changed.

In the years following the accident, I struggled with the shattering impact that fibromyalgia and a mild traumatic brain injury (TBI), caused by the accident, imposed on every aspect of my life. I felt like I was imprisoned in my body, which I dubbed being a "Health Hostage." I lost years of living out my Divine Greatness because I was consumed by the physical symptom management required just to get through the day. As is true for most people with fibromyalgia, I had chronic pain almost 24/7. Overnight I went from being an extraverted person with a very busy, active lifestyle to an extravert trapped in an "introvert's" body. I rarely had the energy to leave the house after a day of work. I experienced loss of restorative sleep on a daily basis; once a sound sleeper, I now regularly had hours of insomnia. I became depressed and hopeless and lost my sense of humour, which was a big part of my personality. My whole social life was in the toilet!

Many of life's challenges offer us the opportunity of transformation, but having a brain injury is not one I ever thought I'd be grateful for. Yet here I write that although my car accident was an enormous life-defining moment, it was not the end of my life. It was only the end of my life as I knew it. This was certainly a loss, and as with any loss there was also grief. But where there is grief, there is also an opportunity to transform loss into love and grief into growth. Over time, I came to recognize this life-defining moment as the beginning of a monumental metamorphosis of self-identity and an opportunity to develop the capacity to love myself unconditionally. Through this journey, I was able to combine my professional skills with my personal experiences. I learned how to use these life-defining moments to shape a new career path of helping others as a loss and transformational grief expert.

Still, even as I went about beginning my new career, I struggled with the sense that I had to hide the truth about myself. As clinicians, we were taught not to be too authentic by sharing our own issues or revealing anything about our private lives to our clients. It can often feel like we are expected to be perfect in order to effectively help our clients. But, just as my entire life had shifted as a result of the car accident, so too did my paradigm for being a perfectionist. With a brain injury and a chronic pain condition, I could no longer perceive myself as perfect. How could I share this new identity and be trusted in my competency as a therapist? I felt shame and fear, and so I kept myself in the closet about it, afraid that others might perceive me as "unfit for duty."

Interestingly enough, it was through a psychologist I sought after my father died who identified that I suffered a mild TBI from my car accident. She was able to do that because *she herself* had a mild TBI and recognized the subtle signs. As a competent and professional psychologist authentically sharing her own journey with a TBI, she gave me the courage to use my personal journey with clients in similar ways.

When I was just restarting my private practice, the first client referred to me was a brain-injury client named Jean, whose regular therapist was retiring. Although this therapist did not really know me, she knew about my car accident and disabilities and told me she referred Jean to me for that very reason. She knew I would "get" Jean and be able to offer her the experience of being understood and seen in a way that only someone with a traumatic brain injury could. While I felt prepared to work with clients again, I did not yet know how much to disclose to this client about my own TBI or anything else, for that matter.

As I explored these questions about self-disclosure and how it may challenge my clinical training, I began to realize there is a difference between a well-trained clinician and a gifted healer. One key element differentiates the two: authenticity. Authenticity is defined as being true to who you are at your core and honest about your own beliefs about yourself and the world. Authenticity is required to be a gifted healer.

So, I began my new practice by modifying the traditional expectations of a "clinician" with those of a gifted healer, and with Jean I started to disclose more of my own history than with any previous clients. Little did I know that one of my life-defining moments would be sharing my own shame about having a TBI while simultaneously being a gifted healer for and with Jean!

I now had an opportunity to redefine my life-defining moment, shifting it from the car accident to a client helping me to shed my own shame. That's truly a life-defining moment when the therapist can thank a client for helping them!

The Sharing of Shame

Sharing shame became part of my methodology for transforming loss into love and grief into growth. Within the construct of the process I entitled "Divine Love is Self-Love" in my book *From Hurting to Healing: 7 Powerful Practices to Manage Your Mind and Heal Your Heart*, shame can find a home to be healed and transformed into self-love. In this process, you work through a series of seven steps which, when repeated as a practice, can start to become your natural and healthy stride. Striding is what happens when you continuously take the steps that will change your mindset and your life. But striding to thrive is not a solitary journey. In fact, the foundational part of success in your thriving is getting and maintaining a good support system. That is exactly what develops in my online programs: a community of people wherein trust is built and the support of everyone makes a positive difference in each person's journey.

This process reminds people that while we may not have been given a choice in having an illness or condition, we do have a choice in how we respond to it. This is a powerful choice because it marks the very fibre of one's being with a prognosis of either healing or suffering. Making this choice can inevitably involve some grief because the choice asks us to confront what has happened to us—confront our shame and bring it out into the open. The grieving process clears the way for self-definition and self-discovery, and with that comes the deep personal growth work that changes who you are and how you live your life.

Perspective is also so important in creating a self-affirming experience. I teach my clients that one powerful way to keep a positive perspective is to practice gratitude. When we practice gratitude, we have an easier time seeing that the glass is half-full. With this mindset, everything becomes possible, because *mindset* determines *everything*.

Conversely, when we create or dwell on negative stories about ourselves (or others) they can impede the forgiveness that is necessary for loving and believing in ourselves and others. These stories manifest in guilt, shame, and blame, which are like poison in our lives, whether we're the ones ingesting it or giving it to others. The best way to free ourselves from debilitating guilt, shame, and blame is to acknowledge the stories that led to them from a truthful point of view and then practice forgiveness and compassion, including self-forgiveness and self-compassion.

To become the person you're meant to be, within the context of your condition, you need to rediscover yourself on a heart and soul level. Once you know your core self, you can begin to envision what your life can be. Then, you'll be able to reinvent your life to make your vision a reality. All of these actions require a strong belief in yourself, your values, and your perseverance. It is all about changing your mindset and your beliefs. In other words, you must rewrite your life story in order to rewire the ways you show up in the world and move yourself from a place of shame to one of self-love and thus reveal your own authenticity. I knew that sharing my own journey with shame, and my healing of that shame, was something I would, at some point, teach Jean.

Sharing Shame with Jean: Making Lemonade Out of Lemons

When Jean started working with me, she was struggling with how to deal with her disabilities. She was very depressed, anxious, and isolated. She lacked a bigger worldview of herself, had low self-esteem, and had no history of self-advocacy or assertiveness. In her own words, "I felt independence before the accident, and afterwards I felt guilty that I couldn't even keep up with friendships much less anything else that resembled who I was. There was so much loss from the accident—my job, my body, my independence. I felt guilt and shame about how disabled I was. I lost a sense of myself, self-confidence, and even the degree of self-love I had before the car accident." Jean did not know how to build a support team and had no toolbox for dealing with her depression, anxiety, and isolation, not to mention her traumatic brain injury. Clueless about how to get past the devastating effects of her car accident, Jean had no idea how to reinvent her life or even how to restart it.

It wasn't too long after beginning our work that I experienced the reciprocity of healing between healer and client as it unfolded one day in a session about shame. Shame is defined as feeling badly about your Self, who you are as a person, as opposed to guilt, which is about behaviour, not Self. And what can be more "shameful" to share than stories of our shame? At least, it can feel that way. But through working with Jean, I developed a different perspective—there is a reciprocity of healing and empowerment when people share their shame.

In one session, I noted that Jean was describing a lot of self-judgment. When I asked her, "Do you feel shame *because* you have a TBI?" her eyes lit up and she exclaimed, "Yes … is that what this is?"

As Jean continued to speak, I recognized what Jean described because I too experienced that for years following my car accident; I too struggled to understand the whole journey of redefining and reinventing myself. I then shared with Jean that at one time, and for a long time, I felt that same shame: I worried about how people perceived me once they knew, and whether it would affect a referral source's or client's trust in me. I talked to her about how I shifted that shame into self-love and self-compassion, that I no longer felt ashamed that I had a TBI, and how I learned to manage my condition and the effects it had on me.

Having experienced disability and my own life and career "derailment" and subsequent reinvention, Jean was an easy client for me to connect with and help. I was able to understand her, but even more importantly, I was able to trust myself because of the success I had in my own healing journey. Had I not already gone down this path of reinvention ahead of Jean, sharing the shame may have not been as professional and therapeutic for either of us. Choosing the right timing for this kind of vulnerability and authenticity is critical to being a gifted healer. The right timing is also critical to the client's experience of their healing journey. Our clients have to know that they can trust us, and they can only do so if we trust ourselves. As Jean explains: "I felt that Nancy's ability to understand what I was going through was stronger for the fact that she had a previous TBI. It meant everything to me that she could even come close to knowing how I'm feeling and could recognize what I am capable of. I very badly needed someone who understood about traumatic brain injuries as I myself did not yet fully understand my own. I thought that since she had lived through it, she would be able to help me live through it also. And that because she rebuilt her life, she could help me rebuild my own."

Within that reciprocity of sharing the shame we felt about having a brain injury was profound healing. I believe it was a life-defining moment for both of us when I helped her identify shame for the first time. It was like a light bulb turned on for her, and she could name shame for what it was. From there, she could begin to understand herself with great clarity. As Jean puts it, "Nancy sharing her shame allowed me to speak about my own, which I didn't even recognize in myself. Part of why I think I had a hard time grieving the car accident and its impact on me was that I had a lot of shame about the TBI and couldn't admit to myself how badly I really was injured. As Nancy helped me to understand my grief and shame and how to deal with it all, I felt a lot of relief and self-compassion." In turn, her gratitude for my sharing and identifying *her* shame was for me a life-defining moment as it enabled me to experience the gift of my own TBI. I was also so proud of myself for all the healing I had done that allowed me to identify it and share with her, bringing her profound healing just in our interactions. That's what I call making lemonade out of lemons.

Jean shared that she had a similar experience of that session: "Nancy identified my shame first, identifying what I was feeling in that moment. And it matched what I was feeling. I really didn't know I was experiencing shame, but it was a terrible feeling. I realized that yes, that was the emotion. And I had carried it with me since the day of the accident. I needed to ask for help but was afraid to let certain people know how bad it truly was. Nancy understood this. It was so powerful that she completely understood everything around this emotion. Then Nancy shared her story about feeling shame that she had a TBI. She identified that I was feeling shame because she recognized that she felt a shame in herself about having a TBI. Nobody talks about the shame. I felt as though I had to keep my TBI a secret. I felt like it's not safe to expose that. Would people still see me as a competent person if they knew?"

As I listened to Jean's feelings of self-doubt and fear of judgment, I reflected back on my own journey and was reminded that, indeed, this is why I remained in the closet of TBI shame. Shame is so powerful, yet sharing shame is even more powerful! Sharing it is the beginning of healing it. It was so gratifying to watch Jean get out of *her* closet of shame just by me sharing *mine*. I know I gave her hope and inspiration. This sharing of shame gave her a cognitive, emotional, and mental framework through which she learned to transform her loss. From there, she could have faith that she could reinvent herself as an artist by using her own TBI journey to eventually return to work through expressive arts, helping others with TBIs if she wanted.

Jean echoes this: "That Nancy was able to be vulnerable enough to share her shame helped me see that I could get past it too. I could see that while she understood the shame, she was not affected by it. That she understood it and saw how it affected her life and wasn't trapped by it. She felt completely comfortable sharing what she went through. In this I could see that I could learn to recognize my shame, when I felt it, and not be triggered by it or hide myself away."

Feeling shame is the antithesis of unconditional self-love. Unconditional self-love, at its deepest level, reflects our most authentic self, the experience of oneself as Divine Love. The authentic sharing of my own shame allowed Jean and I to reframe sharing shame as a pathway to self-love and self-compassion and to feel the liberation of coming out of the closet. This moment became yet another "redefining-the-life-defining moment" for me as well as for Jean.

Being authentic with clients means we share aspects of ourselves when it is in the service of our clients, not ourselves. Knowing when and how to share your authenticity is again part of what makes one a gifted healer. When clients struggle with being authentic due to lack of self-esteem or fear of judgment from others, sharing our authentic selves offers our clients the opportunity to feel safe doing that as well.

Since none of us are perfect, being a whole, integrated person is about loving the good, the bad, and the ugly about yourself; at your very core is love of all these parts of Self. That is the definition of *unconditional* self-love. When we are authentic, we invite others to be the same: to love themselves unconditionally. *It is that very love that dissolves shame.*

The Journey of the Caterpillar

Life-defining moments often remind me of the transformational journey of a caterpillar who ultimately turns into a butterfly. The caterpillar's Divine Greatness is to transform into a butterfly. How this transformation happens is very pivotal to the concept of the struggle and pain of "shedding" a part of itself to become a butterfly. Simply, a caterpillar cannot become a butterfly without first being a caterpillar and going through the struggle of freeing itself of its previous "identity."

And so it seems that struggle is inherent in everyone's path to unfolding their greatness.

Can we learn from the caterpillar about changing one's form/identity, about the experience of struggle and instinctual "rejection" of what one is at the moment? Can we then believe that the outcome of "shedding" one's old self leads to transformation?

Coming Out of the Closet of Shame

Shame may feel like you are wandering around in a no-man's-land. It may feel hard, it may feel scary, it may even feel dangerous to share your shame. But ultimately sharing shame brings freedom to how you experience yourself in relationship to the world.

Shame, by its very nature, is isolating because we are prone to keep it a secret. Keeping the secret of shame protects you from the possibility of judgment and rejection from others, which you may fear. Unfortunately, the danger in keeping shame a secret is that it isolates you *from yourself* as well as from others. The isolation *only serves to maintain your shame*. Staying in that closet of shame prohibits you from experiencing unconditional self-love. Therefore, it is hard to heal shame by yourself! That's a conundrum, isn't it? Only not really, once we realize it is actually through the very act of sharing shame that we can begin our healing and are on the path toward unconditional self-love. That is a huge payoff for exiting the closet of shame!

Once we start on our path of self-love, we open ourselves to making new connections around the original sources of our shame. Talking with Jean about our work together, she recalls times when we burst out laughing about shared experiences with having a TBI. "We would joke that we have one person with a TBI leading another," Jean says. "We were able to laugh about certain things like forgetfulness and such. This is the first time I could even joke or laugh about having a TBI. After not being understood by doctors and not given much help outside of the Acquired Brain Injury classes on how to deal with a TBI, I had not had any laughter about it, that's for sure." To take a complex issue and laugh about it with someone who intimately knows it from the inside out is, in Jean's words, extraordinary.

By shifting our perspectives in this way, these obstacles, much like the walls of a caterpillar's cocoon, become life-defining opportunities to free yourself from the confines of that cocoon and fly to your greatest heights of unconditional self-love, *where shame can no longer abide.*

It is time now in our work with clients to consider the profound benefits of reciprocity between client and therapist. I have found that being authentic with my clients engenders trust and the example that it is safe to be ourselves and to be seen.

Our authenticity provides our clients with a model for how to identify and experience self-love. Jean notes that, "The whole thing about shame is that it never gets talked about. I suppose Nancy trusted me enough to be vulnerable to share her own shame with me. It's pretty crazy amazing that the healer can be healed in the reciprocity of healing another person. Usually, this openness is not what is practiced in a medical transaction. As a client, I find it really beautiful to know that I have the power to heal an experienced healer."

Epilogue

When I was invited by Jennifer Nagel to contribute a chapter to this collaborative book, I knew immediately what I would write about, and about which client. It was a "no brainer" (pun intended) to use this opportunity to break out of the closet of shame. However, as a therapist/coach, it still felt like a daring risk to talk about shame in a book and tell the world I experienced a brain injury. I felt a few moments of fear, but eventually I realized that in the very vulnerable act of taking this risk, I was practicing what I preach: sharing shame provides a vehicle toward healing in and of itself. And besides, don't we all experience shame about something at one time or another?

I could have chosen other topics and other clients, but my highest mission in life is to make a difference in the world, to make a difference in others' quality of life and self-expression. Most of all, I am dedicated to being a light in the world and to lifting up others. To me, the highest service I can offer anyone is to help them as my authentic self. My mission to uplift others happens deeply when we share our shame, because it is only then that we can all begin to experience unconditional self-love. And self-love means Divine Love, which is our true nature.

Jean and I were (and are) still working together when I told her I was writing a chapter for a book about reciprocity in healing relationships. When I asked her how she would feel if I wrote about our working relationship and our TBIs, Jean teared up and expressed that she would be honoured to have her story included. "I can feel very small at times," she explained. "You help me see that I am not small, and that I am very capable, even with the disabilities I have. I still want to make a difference in this world. And being asked to use my story, *me*, just being me, with injuries and disabilities, makes me feel not small but big. To realize that just being myself can help others was a very new idea, and it makes me so happy that I can contribute."

The feeling of being honoured is a signal that one is on a journey of self-love and that others are able to recognize and support it. I was so honoured that Jean felt good about herself and our work together. By empowering her to share her story, I was, in fact, uplifting Jean and myself in that process! There is such reciprocity of feeling good and loving yourself and loving others in that kind of exchange. I always write on Jean's invoices "It is a joy and honour to work with you, Jean," and now I can add a gratitude to that list too.

About Nancy M. Gordon

Nancy M. Gordon, LCSW, CLC, is a #1 international best-selling author, consultant, speaker, and life-changing expert who knows firsthand what it's like to deal with serious loss and grief after a devastating car accident. In her upcoming teaching memoirs, *7 Steps of Hope: Healing the Emotional, Mental, and Spiritual Impacts of Chronic Illness and Disability, 7 Powerful Practices to Manage Your Mind and Heal Your Heart*, and *I Miss You Already: Bearing the Unbearable Loss of Your Pet*, Nancy combines her professional expertise and personal experience with fibromyalgia and a mild traumatic brain injury to offer a unique perspective on how to transform loss into love and grief into growth through hope and healing with wit and wisdom. Her work is endorsed by Dr. Karen Becker, a leading veterinarian and a *New York Times* best-selling author.

As a well-known loss and transformational grief expert and educator, Nancy's media presence includes television, radio/podcast interviews, magazines, and books. Nancy lives in San Diego, California, where she enjoys swimming, being in nature, and writing.

www.linkedin.com/in/nancygordon7stepsofhope/
linktr.ee/nancygordonglobal
www.instagram.com/nancy.gordon.global/
www.facebook.com/NGordonGlobal
www.nancygordonglobal.com

5

Baby Samuel and Me: Stories of Adoption Across Generations

By Tami Blackwell Jennings

Nothing you do for children is ever wasted.

— **Garrison Keillor**

Baby Samuel and Me:
Stories of Adoption Across Generations

By Tami Blackwell Jennings

This chapter is dedicated to my big sister, Debbie. Thank you for mentoring me all my life with patience, love, and unending generosity. I will forever be grateful to you! And, for my chosen sisters, dearest of friends and kindred spirits for life, my Golden Girls: Bonnie, Rhonda, and Denise … Each of you are a cherished gift. Thank you for loving me unconditionally for all these years. I end this chapter with deep gratitude for my little sister, Amy, who contacted me two days after I returned from Mexico after years of hoping to find a biological relative. Her presence has solved the mystery of who I really am and has given me a sense of peace I never had before.

* * *

Most college graduates enter the field of social work with the hope they can make a difference in people's lives. They want to make life better for the families and individuals they serve. After a few months of working in Indian Child Welfare, I realized it was a steep uphill battle to really help in a significant way. Over the years, the families on my client list either welcomed me into their lives or did everything they could to avoid me at all costs. We all have our stories of best and worst experiences. Here are two of my most memorable experiences. One, scary and unsuccessful, the other, a story of faith and hope that impacted me so deeply I became forever grateful to my own family.

My social working career began in a unit called the County Prevention Program. We were assigned clients who needed assistance with parenting through life's difficulties. Offering emergency services such as groceries, formula, diapers, clothing, and even furniture, we tried to provide for our families what they could not attain for themselves. Announced visits usually begin well, as the family makes an appointment for the worker to come to their home and they understand the reason behind the visit. Unannounced visits almost always begin with clients in a defensive mode, feeling angry and suspicious of whoever knocks on their door.

My new clients were a family of four whose three-year-old daughter had been diagnosed as morbidly obese by a nurse at the state's family services program: Women, Infants, and Children. Her one-year-old little sister was on the same path to obesity. I was to educate the parents about healthy food choices for themselves and their girls. Initially I felt confident as I had a nutrition background, but from my car I could see the porch was littered with stacks of old pizza boxes and plastic trash bags full of empty soda bottles. Walking up the steps and looking around the front porch, I realized this unannounced home visit may not go well, but I still had hope.

As soon as I knocked on the door, my confidence completely evaporated … I felt only doubt and fear. That knock resulted in maniacal barking from what must've been a very large dog. It began hurling its body against the door and I thought it might come off its hinges. Gratefully, the dog's owners did not seem to be home. Breathing a sigh of relief, I prepared to leave the required message that I had attempted to visit and requested a return phone call. Now I could return to the safety of my office. No such luck! A deep gravelly voice called out: "Hang on and let me put this @#*%! dog up!" I could hear cursing and nails scraping the floor as the dog was dragged away. After several minutes the barking faded and I could hear, and feel, heavy footsteps crossing the wood floor. The door opened a crack, and I carefully pushed my business card through, identifying myself as her family's assigned tribal social worker in connection to Indian Child Welfare. Opening further revealed an extremely large woman who had a decidedly unfriendly and suspicious expression on her face. However, she allowed me to step in, with me quickly explaining to her the reason for my visit. This caused her eyes to bulge out and her face became very red. Somehow she swallowed her anger and asked me to sit down. She was calm but clearly shocked that anyone would classify her little girl as morbidly obese, when in her opinion she was just "big" like the rest of the family.

Over the next twelve weeks I tried to impress upon mom and dad that their children's health was dependent on the quality of foods they ate. I provided health department brochures, articles on healthy foods for children, and recipe books, all extolling the virtues of good nutrition. The parents graciously endured my visits yet made no significant change in their diets. The ferocious dog, an enormous male pit bull who eventually was released from a back room, crept closer to me on each visit. He decided I was a friend and on my very last visit climbed on my lap and bathed my ear with slobbery kisses.

Because of my middle-class upbringing by my close-knit, hard-working family, most of my visits to clients were real eye-openers. The poverty level was high and most of my families lived a spartan existence with very little money and few belongings. I struggled with the feeling that I could never do enough for my families. They needed so much, and I had no way to provide most of what they needed. It was sad and frustrating. But, the people became very dear to me. I was proud of them for their tenacity in attempting to rise above the situation they had been in. And, no matter the issue or reason behind my visit, the parents loved their children unconditionally. Family was the most important part of their culture and their lives.

A few years later I was invited to a different child welfare unit: Adoption and Foster Care. This was exciting as I had been adopted myself and I looked forward to helping tribal families jump through all the hoops to get placement of a child. My job was to take a family's application, visit several times, advise them on creating their profile book, develop their home safety plans, and complete their home study. I loved being a part of many happy endings, but none were as meaningful to me as the adoption of one very special baby boy.

Over many weeks, I visited the Barrett family several times and was impressed with their strong commitment to adopt a child, their extended family's desire to support them, and the efficiency and speed in which they readied their home for their final visit and home study. Emily and Robert Barrett were both educated, owned their own business, and were devoted to their faith. Emily was prepared to become a stay-at-home mom as soon as a baby was placed with them. Several months passed and they began to worry that a birth mother would not pick them to be their child's forever family. They were older, Emily in her late thirties and Rob in his early forties, and most birth moms were quite young, making the couple the age of a baby's biological grandparents.

One morning I received a call from Emily. The enthusiasm in her voice told me something was up. She excitedly asked if I could come to the hospital as a birth mother had picked them from the profile book and the baby boy had arrived in the early hours that morning.

Later that day I arrived at the hospital, expecting to see the new parents and the baby. Emily and Rob were in the hospital room, joined by Emily's parents, but no baby boy. They reported he was being treated with an IV infusion in the nursery as he was born with alcohol in his system. It turned out the birth mom had had only one month of sobriety during pregnancy and it was in her fifth month when she had lived with her father. This was devastating news for the baby. The odds of fetal alcohol syndrome (FAS) were high. Yet, no one could predict the outcome. When I later held the tiny infant, I was taken with how beautiful he was. Even so, I searched his face for the classic physical signs of FAS: a small head, small eyes, an extra fold in the inner corner of the eye, a flat nasal bridge, a flat area between tip of the nose and where the Cupid's bow of the top lip should be, and a very thin upper lip. I saw none of these signs.

The Barretts told me they had prayed unceasingly from the time they received the call until their arrival at the hospital several hours later. They had their large extended family, church, and community praying for the baby's health. They were committed to adopting him regardless of whether the doctors suspected FAS.

On the drive to the hospital, they had discussed a good name for the boy. Rob said he had a name in mind but wanted to know if Emily had thought of one. She told him Samuel, as it was from one of her favourite stories in the Bible. Rob looked at her in amazement and said that Samuel was the very name he had thought of! When they arrived at the hospital, they were able to meet the birth mother.

They knew it was no coincidence when she asked if they would consider giving her son the name she had chosen—Samuel!

Even though they had already decided to adopt the baby, they asked for my opinion. Although I was afraid of the difficulties and struggles they may endure if Samuel had FAS, I had to say that I thought they should move forward with the adoption. I couldn't let my fears cloud the possibility that Samuel just might be okay. This was because of the stories my parents had told me of my own adoption.

In the year I was born, if a teenage girl became pregnant she was sent to live with relatives or at an unwed mothers' home, generally called a maternity home, to have her baby and give it up for adoption. The pregnancy and birth were usually kept secret, and afterward the teen was expected to return home and step back into her former life as if nothing had happened. Giving birth is an experience no woman can forget, so to keep it a secret has to be heartbreaking.

My parents had been married several years when they found out they could not have their own children. They both had siblings, all married and with families. They were the favourite aunt and uncle to all their nieces and nephews. They had good jobs, had purchased their first home, and decided it was time … they would try to adopt a baby. They were assigned a social worker and accomplished all the steps in preparation for their home study. After six months they joyfully received placement of their first daughter, and a year later formally adopted her. This little girl who would become my older sister was adorable, calm, and happy. She fit right into their schedule, sleeping through the night, waking late in the morning with her mother, and staying up until her parents went to bed. They were a family! Two and a half years later, they came home to a note from their social worker stuck on their mailbox. It said: "Good news! Call me!" I had arrived and had been matched with them. They travelled back to the same maternity home to meet me. Even though I was a "failure to thrive" baby, they said "yes" to adopting me. They could not take me home that day, as it was mandatory for a baby to stay in the home for six weeks before being placed.

At that time, much was being learned about child development, but doctors were just becoming aware of how much a newborn baby needed to be held and interacted with. The first weeks of my life were spent in a bassinet; I was only held when fed and was mostly likely in discomfort, as I was allergic to the homemade cow's milk formulas used then. At six weeks I was brought home by my parents. My arrival was just as excitedly anticipated as any biological child could have been: the entire extended family celebrated. Although my sister Debbie was not biological, she was always my big sister and I thought she hung the moon.

Samuel's experience was quite different from mine. During all the tests and medical treatment, he was rocked, spoken and sung to, and patted, and every need, both physical and emotional, was met. Emily and Rob stayed in a hospital room with him while he was treated and actually detoxed until his system was considered free of alcohol. They were able to take him home when he was three days old. Although closely monitored, Samuel was with family from the time he was born.

The first six weeks of my life undoubtedly had an effect on me. Although I was never very comfortable with physical affection and had not been held much, as a grown up I never thought of myself as having had an attachment disorder. More interaction during my first weeks of life before placement might have helped me meet my developmental milestones, but there is no way to know for sure. My parents were loving, and while they didn't express their love with a lot of kisses and hugs, I know they held and rocked me. They figured out very quickly that I needed to be fed something other than cow's milk and started using goat's milk to make my formula. I began to gain weight and really thrive. I was a happy baby, and my parents were completely focused on my sister and me.

Still, it soon became obvious I was different from my big sister. I needed little sleep and woke up very early, so at night I went to bed very early. My parents' schedule was turned upside down! As I grew older, those differences became even more apparent. I was "that child," the one standing fearlessly on the top bar of the swing set. Climbing the shelves in Sunday school to get a snack, only to have the shelves topple over with a loud crash. I can only imagine my parents' embarrassment when one day the neighbour casually remarked that they were enjoying my company each morning at breakfast. Always an early riser, I had been leaving the house in the early morning darkness, eating with the neighbour, and returning home without my parents having a clue!

Those calm, quiet days before I arrived were long gone. I was talking, singing, dancing, and telling stories constantly. All of this must have been hard on my sister as well. I was a major annoyance to her peace-loving soul. In our early days, she quietly avoided me and when at all possible stayed in her room. I grew to want to please her so she would spend time with me. I wanted to be just like her.

I'm amazed to this day that my parents never compared me to my bright and beautiful sister. She excelled academically and socially. I saw her as perfect and as everything I was not. Despite all our differences, she seemed to sense when I didn't feel capable, and she encouraged me and expected the best from me. When I struggled, she told me of her own struggles in learning to study effectively. She was sharp-witted, honest, brave, tenacious, studious, smart, and classy. She knew how to have fun and be a good friend and was the most generous person I knew. She was an excellent mentor for her funny little sister who definitely marched to the beat of a different drummer!

Although there were developmental terms such as "hyperactive," I don't remember hearing anyone using that word while I was growing up. I also didn't hear the terms "processing issues" or "developmental delays." However, all of my caregivers and teachers said I was "very active." Every report card said: "Tami doesn't listen, doesn't sit still, has a short attention span, doesn't complete her assignments, and talks too much." I was hyperactive all right!

School was not a happy place for me. I felt out of place and like I could never quite "get" what the teacher was trying to explain. I never felt that my teachers liked me. My entire fifth-grade year was spent sitting at a desk wedged in the front corner of the classroom with my back to the other students. It began the very first day, which let me know my reputation had preceded me. Thankfully I was a good reader on my own, and I believe it was because my parents read to my sister and me and provided many good children's books for us to read.

Before I understood being adopted was different, I told a friend at school how my parents got me. I'm sure my parents didn't tell me this, but I believed I was in a room full of babies in bassinets and my parents came in, looked at all the babies, and picked me! That's how special they made me feel. (As an adult looking at the picture of my mom holding me in the maternity home, I knew this could not be so! I was born breech, so my head was round and looked enormous compared to my spindly arms and legs. I was not an adorable baby with curly hair and dimples!) Well, this friend whom I had shared my adoption story with spread the word to other classmates. One day on the playground a big boy began taunting me, and the other children circled around me. He said: "You were adopted! Your own mom and dad didn't want you!" I was crushed. It had never occurred to me that my birth parents didn't want me. For the first time in my life, I knew what rejection felt like, and it did not feel good. It wasn't until after I had my first baby that I realized there had to be different reasons for my biological parents placing me for adoption. It wasn't because they didn't want me. That feeling of rejection lessened more and more as I raised my own family. I just knew there had to be more to the story.

I seemed to catch up academically to everyone else after junior high. Even though I struggled to feel accepted and "normal" and had never developed good self-esteem, I slowly became successful in many ways. Pure and simple, this was because my parents gave me so many great experiences in life. They provided physical activities, bicycles, scooters, and skates, and moved to a house a half a block from a swimming pool. I was able to use all my excess energy in positive ways. We always had pets in our home, but our lives really changed when my sister fell in love with horses. My parents paid for riding lessons for both of us and eventually bought us our own horse and all the tack and equipment to travel to horse shows and fox hunts. I stayed at the barn for as long as I could and loved every minute of it. Becoming successful as a rider and winning competitions was a balm to my soul. For many years, my parents donated all of their earnings, evenings, weekends, and vacation days to our horse competitions. My parents were completely devoted to giving us our best life.

Samuel's adoption reminded me of my own, with a rough beginning, hopeful parents, and a good outcome. But, adoption doesn't always have a happy ending. Within Indian Child Welfare, tribal policy for foster care and especially adoption is to be "family first." If the birth mother or birth father is unable to care for their baby, the tribe searches diligently for members of the immediate family to take placement. This is often good as it gives the birth parents a chance to work on a plan of recovery in the case of alcohol or drug addiction, and gives parents who simply need to find a job or housing more time to do so. Sometimes, however, it is not a good placement for the baby. Often, if the birth parent has substance abuse issues, it has been a part of their family history, and the older generation's environment is not any better than that of the parents. If a family has three strikes against them and cannot stay sober, keep a job, or attain a safe environment, the baby will be placed elsewhere. It's a difficult job for a social worker to assess the physical safety of a home. Even more difficult to assess if the emotional environment of the home is appropriate and nurturing for a growing child.

Six months after the Barretts took Samuel home from the hospital, they formally adopted him. I was thrilled to be able to attend Samuel's final adoption proceedings with the Barretts and their large extended family. It was a joyous experience! Two years later, I left social work to continue my career in child nutrition. Although I am no longer a social worker, I follow the Barrett family through social media and we exchange occasional messages. Samuel is now a healthy, happy boy, loving his family and church, with many close friends and loved ones surrounding him. Unlike when I was a child, adoption is now considered quite commonplace and looked upon as a positive thing. My prayer is that Samuel will never be bullied or belittled for being an adopted child.

A long-forgotten memory came to me while I was the Barrett family's social worker. Emily's parents, Grace and William, had been at their home during one of my visits. They spoke of the extended family's excitement about Rob and Emily's new baby. They were completely accepting of adoption even though they were of a generation where adoption was often looked at as shameful. Since adoptable infants generally came from "broken homes" or unwed mothers, adopted children were considered lower class. In my own life, I had always been surrounded by a loving extended family and treated as an equal ... I was just one of the family. But, one day an older sister of my mother's came to visit for a week close to Christmas. She lived in Texas, and we rarely saw her. I was a young mother and had been working diligently on handmade gifts for my mom and dad. I was excited to show her my handiwork. I took her into a bedroom where I had hidden two cross-stitched pillows: I had stitched a mother and father poem on each and used coordinating colours to match their bedroom decor. My aunt admired them and said, "These are beautiful! But I'm really surprised you made them for your parents." This made no sense to me, so I asked her why. She said, "Well, because you are adopted and I never imagined you would feel this way toward them." This made me realize, probably for the first time in my life, how people who have had no experience with an adopted child or family see adoption from the outside. They just cannot understand how anyone could love a child that is not a biological part of themselves nor how a child could love their adoptive parents.

Yet, I knew from a six-week-old baby's perspective that my mother and father cared for me and loved me. The peace and tranquility of unconditional love is palpable. I felt it. All my life I knew it way down inside of my soul.

Watching the Barrett family begin their journey with such unwavering faith continued to remind me of my own family. Their prayers, and the prayers of all of those around them … their belief that we would be healthy and whole, made it so. Both my family and Samuel's were prepared to love their children through any hardship and were willing to sacrifice to help us become successful. I am very grateful I was able to be a part of the Barretts' adoption process. Seeing their story unfold helped me to accept my own adoption. It solidified my belief that even though my birth and adoption make me different, it is a good difference. I believe I am enough. I believe in myself and my value to others in my life. Truly, there are no coincidences. I was supposed to be adopted by my parents. I was supposed to be placed with my sister. I was *wanted* and considered a priceless gift by my family.

When my mother was in her eighties, she and I chatted about when she was a young mother. She always said the days she was a stay-at-home mom with my sister and me were some of her favourites: She loved having her babies home and being a mom. We reminisced, recalling our best funny family stories and laughing. My mother was a positive and upbeat person, and she rarely complained, but then the subject turned to my early years and some of my more famous "antics." She agreed I was a challenge … and added, "Oh dear, if we'd gotten you first, we would have never gotten more children!" We laughed together, but it made me realize just how tough parenting me must have been. Yet, I knew she and my dad had loved me with their whole hearts, completely and unconditionally!

Being a part of Samuel's adoption gave me a better understanding of what a life-changing decision my parents made for me. My birth mother must have loved me very much to have given me up for adoption. She gave me a chance to be raised by a family who were mature and ready to devote their lives to a child. On the other hand, my adoptive parents took me home suspecting I had some issues yet nurtured me for the rest of their lives. They never wavered in their devotion and support. I will forever be indebted to my mom, dad, sister, and extended family for making my life the best it could be!

Epilogue

When I chose to write of my experience with baby Samuel and how it had impacted my life, I knew it was the right story to share. The similarity of his story to mine had prompted me to reflect on my own life in important ways. Still, I wondered about my birth mother and family. Samuel's adoptive parents had met his birth mother. They had been given family medical history and heard his mother's dreams and desires for her baby. In the state where I was born, adoption records are still closed. Even if an adoptee wanted to reach out, it was impossible to find any biological relatives … until DNA analysis companies such as Ancestry.com and 23andMe were born.

Two days after returning from Puerto Vallarta, Mexico, I was back at work, hurrying to catch up on emails, phone calls, and staffing issues. My heart remained at the Casa de Influencia creative retreat, and my mind kept returning to the memories of the marvelous people I had spent the week learning from. I had written the first draft of my contribution for this book and was happy with the results. Midmorning I had made progress on catching up on tasks but needed to finish up to attend an administrative meeting. As I rose from my chair, my computer pinged to notify me a new email had arrived. I hesitated and looked to see who it was from. Oh, it was just 23andMe, one of the many requests to participate in DNA studies. With no family history, I was never able to participate in any studies, so I automatically reached to delete it. Instead, the subject line grabbed my interest, and I caught my breath. It was from a new relative.… I clicked on it and read: "Hi Tami! I was shocked to find out I have a sister! I thought I had more half-siblings than I was aware of but never in a million years would have thought this was possible. I am sad I missed growing up with you & don't understand why I didn't. Sadly, I don't think there is anyone alive that would know. I have sent a message to a cousin & haven't heard back. I hope you had a better childhood than I did. I'd love to hear back from you. – Amy."

I ran to my meeting but heard little of anything said. I was stunned, and absolutely thrilled.… All these years hoping and praying to find a biological relative and suddenly I had a sister!

It has been two weeks, and Amy and I have emailed and texted back and forth. She has sent me numerous pictures and described our parents and half-siblings. She and I resemble each other in looks and have many of the same characteristics. I cannot wait to meet her face to face! Between spending a week with a dear friend and nine wonderful co-writers, and finding my sister Amy, I have a new peace within me. There is a feeling of happiness and contentment I have never experienced before. I know who I am and where I came from.

However, my adoptive mom, dad, and sister will always be my "real family." They loved and believed in me first, and I will always be grateful to them.

P.S.

Two weeks after finishing this chapter, my friend Rhonda and I travelled to Ohio to meet my sister in person. We met Amy and her best friend Debra, and the four of us had a wonderful time together. Amy and I are so alike in so many ways: looks, interests, and abilities … it's amazing to me! We have plans to meet again soon, but the best part of it all is that Amy will be travelling to Casa de Influencia in Puerta Vallarta for our book launch! A huge thank you to the retreat's wonderfully supportive writing collaborators and editors. We will share the outcome of this journey from the beginning (i.e., the great unknown) to my and Amy's reunion … a new beginning to the rest of our story.

About Tami Blackwell Jennings

Tami Blackwell Jennings, BS, BHRS, is a Child Nutrition Director for a large rural school district and a volunteer teacher for women in recovery. Through her work, she provides nutritional choices and education for healthy living for students as well as staff. She continues to expand her influence through working with legislators on the state level for a healthier future beginning with the school systems. Tami transitioned from using her skills as a social worker with the foster and adoption program in Indian Child Welfare to impacting the lives of women returning to the community after spending time in rehabilitation programs and prison. She joins them in their journey of learning to live a healthy, fulfilling life through faith, and she teaches communication, personal growth, and relapse prevention. Tami is very passionate about community building and connections. She is proud to work with a diverse range of students, staff, administrators, and legislators, as well as women in recovery. She seeks to do her part in making the world a better place.

www.facebook.com/tami.jennings.71

6

A Promise to a Baby, A Gift from the Creator

By Shelley J. Cook

*The quality of life for many
may depend on you.
Go and make a difference.
The whole world waits for you.*

— Chief Robert Joseph

A Promise to a Baby, A Gift from the Creator

By Shelley J. Cook

I have decided to listen to Spirit and others who have told me to take a leap and write! I am going to write about some things I have grown to be comfortable with in myself, but which I am still not so comfortable sharing outwardly. Yet, medicine can be found in the most unexpected of places. In life's most difficult moments. In times of grief and heartache. In the hardest decisions we will ever make. It is in those moments that promises are real and made from the Soul. Gifts from the Spirit come to us to help us continue on our paths. By writing this chapter, I am going to serve myself first. In giving myself the gift of permission, truth, creativity, and self-expression, I also give it to you. I welcome you to join me on this journey in experiencing this gift.

A Promise and a Gift

I feel as if I am a witness to my own life at times. Like I am watching it. Sometimes it's hard as hell when I am in it, and other times it is graceful and easy. I love the graceful times.

What I know now, and have known for a long time, is that when I help others, it's the easiest part of my life. I just know how to help. I love big, and helping comes effortlessly to me.

I'm a mother of five sons, and I believe I am a good mom. But, I am not always good at it. It doesn't always come so easy to me. Still, loving my sons has always been easy. I love my sons, I care for them, and I nurture them. I discipline them in a stronger, stiffer kind of way. I feel I am a masculine mom, for the most part. I am not the feminine mom who becomes a pretend ambulance when her child falls down, making the sounds to go with it to fix their "booboos." To me, that kind of sweet nurturing is the realm of a feminine mother.

I am a Native woman who lives on an Indian reservation of the 'Namgis. We are of the Kwakwa̱ka'wakw Nation. Our people speak Kwak'wala. We are now situated in Alert Bay on a little island, five miles around, called Cormorant Island, in British Columbia, Canada. It was once a booming logging and commercial fishing community. My dad was a skipper, and I started working with him when I was thirteen, first in the salmon industry and then in later years the herring industry up and down the coast.

In 1993, I was twenty-five. I had three sons when I got pregnant again in March. At the time, life had many challenges. My partner was peaking in his use of alcohol and drugs, his binge drinking turning into drug binges. It was a struggle to keep the house going, to stay on top of the bills with all his money going to his addictions, and to answer my sons' questions about where their dad was. I didn't lie, but I was running out of ways to explain his absence.

As a teenager and young adult, I knew I would always keep and raise my sons no matter what—and I did. As March rolled into April, I became sick. Morning sickness. I had some decisions to make. I went to see the doctor a couple weeks later to confirm I was pregnant. Tracked down the dad to tell him. I don't remember too many details, but I do remember that I told him I thought we needed to abort the baby. I didn't know how I could bring another child into the chaos in which we were living in: it was rough and unpredictable, with lots of violence.

He was emotional. I was emotional. I didn't see another way at the time. I had my hands full with my three sons. Their quality of life was not what they deserved—I wanted to do better for them. I knew it wouldn't be fair to bring another baby in and not be able to give it what it needed.

After that moment of telling him I was pregnant, the dad continued on his binge. I didn't see him for almost a month. I was so angry, frustrated, and overwhelmed. Out of hopelessness I booked an abortion. It broke my heart! At the time, I could not see another way through. I was crushed in every way. As far back as I could remember, abortion was something I told myself and my sisters I would never do. Abortion would never be an option for me.

The appointment to terminate the baby, which is what they called it, was the Thursday before Mother's Day. I went to the pre-op appointment to prepare for the next day. The appointment is to make sure you have no reservations. The doctor did a procedure where she puts a sponge in the uterus to absorb the liquid of the fetus, to help make the actual procedure easy. It was an awful experience.

I no longer completely remember what happened after that, but I do remember going to the hospital the next day. The doctor had to deliver two emergency babies, so from seven in the morning I had to sit in the waiting room for hours, in a gown. The dad was with me. He asked me a couple times if we should just get up and run! I was tempted every time. But my body wasn't able to move.

When the doctor finally showed up, she and an assistant brought me down the hallway on a gurney through these doors. Very dramatic. Had last words with the dad. Then they left me in a hallway for what seemed like forever. I was in a hallway where they stored the hospital linens on rows of metal shelves.

I was all alone, in a hospital hallway, a scene from a horror movie. My horror movie. I sobbed, and at times when I knew I was alone, I would begin to wail. I prayed and prayed! I talked to the Gods! I don't remember having faith back then, not like I do now. It was painful! It actually felt like my heart was tearing, being shredded apart. It was emotionally and physically painful. In the time I was there, I talked to God and to the baby, asking for forgiveness. I repeatedly said sorry. Sorry I wasn't enough to raise another baby on my own. Then the doctor showed up. I sat up like a shot! I said, "Hey doctor … how is the baby? Is it too late?" She grabbed my hand and said, "It isn't a baby yet, it's called a fetus. We put the sponge in the cervix to absorb the fluid around the fetus. There's no way of knowing its status, unless we do an ultrasound to find out." She said it coldly, but as sensitively as she could. She was behind schedule, so she was matter-of-fact, moving fast to get me in and done. I hated her! How dare she disregard my baby like that!

My heart broke to a new low. I cried so hard. If she had said the baby would be fine, I would have jumped up and run off and never looked back. When she was gone, I knew the damage had already been done to the fetus and I couldn't go back. I did this; I made this choice. All that was left for me to do was make promises to my child, to remember the promises and work hard to keep them.

So I made promises! Promises to my child! Promises to God! I needed a big, huge promise, something that matched the value of a life. I promised that this was not just going to be a tragedy! The child's brief life would not be for nothing! I would not waste its life for nothing! This was going to be a turning point in my life. I was going to do good, do great things with my life! I would do great things with my life from now on.

This was all I could do! So I promised, and I didn't just say it to say it, I meant it, every word of it. I absolutely meant it with all my heart and Soul. Even though I didn't know how I was going to keep my promise or what it would even mean for my life, I meant it!

I never forgot my promise. Life continued. We went fishing and the same ol' same ol' went on. Yet, I was a tormented soul! I had known that I wouldn't be able to live with my decision. I began self-destructing. The dad blamed me, and so did I. We blamed each other and took revenge, fighting and being cruel.

Somehow, I don't remember how it came to be, but I got the idea to go to Nanaimo to attend a Counselling Teacher Aide program at the Tillicum Lelum Aboriginal Friendship Centre. To attend these programs, you had to have a certain amount of sobriety. I applied; they accepted me. I remembered my promise. I made the choice to leave the dad behind in the Bay. I took my sons with me. This was a bone of contention. But, I strongly felt it had to be this way in order for me to succeed. In order to make the changes I knew I had to make, I couldn't bring him and his chaos with me.

My sons and I moved to Nanaimo. It was a big deal. I had never lived anywhere but Alert Bay. Little girl from the Rez taking three young sons to the city. It was no small thing. Holy, the city—city for us. Making our way around, seven of us in my mom's five-seater car. It took a lot for me to get schools and daycares set up for the boys, still in my heartbreak. I was so sad and hurt. The grief hurt. Once everyone got settled, I started to mend my broken heart.

The counselling program was like a year of treatment. The way the instructors taught us, we got our training by working through our own healing process. It was intense. We learned through self-awareness, through taking accountability for our own lives. There was no getting away from my decision to abort my child, and now I had to find a way to live with it. Even as I seemed to make progress on the outside, on the inside I was shrivelling up.

I didn't know it then, but the program was the perfect place for me to be. They brought in many teachers, facilitators, coaches, seers, and healers to teach and train us. They brought a man who did exorcisms, people who helped you heal up family systems, traumas, and things like past lives so you could release the patterns that had been holding you back in this lifetime. It blew my mind, blew it right open! What I was learning, I already intuitively knew, but now they were giving me the words for it. They were giving me the words for this knowing I had. I did many processes about the baby and bawled every time. I had returned the baby to the Creator by aborting it, and through this work I was fully giving it back to the Creator. Through the tears, I was releasing the baby, letting it free, and, in the process, learning to forgive myself.

Over that year, there were many steps, so many layers of healing I had to work through around the abortion and the life I was dealt. I had to come to the place of helping myself! I had felt I wasn't worthy of healing because I had brought it all on myself, through my own actions. I thought I had no choice but to swallow the pain. Yet, once I made the choice to help myself with the help of the facilitators, I started to navigate the suffering.

After I completed that program, I took the Drug and Alcohol Counsellor program they offered. That was when I really turned the corner. I was able to make space in me to let some light, some love, in the small cracks where my heart was broken.

I worked with a seer who helped me understand things more clearly. She helped me see what the agreement between the baby and me was all about. She said that I had an agreement with this Spirit (baby) to come in later in my life to plant a "gift" in me. To bring me a Spiritual Gift to help others. If I had been born with this gift, it would have been detrimental to me. I would have been so open and sensitive that it would have caused me immense pain and suffering. It would have been too painful for a child to live with—I would not have survived. The agreement was for the Spirit to come, plant the gift, and leave shortly after being conceived. The seer explained that the baby was never meant to stay to full term because its purpose was to deliver the gift and go back to the spirit world. I agreed to have this gift to help others. To raise the consciousness of many people.

Everything she said rang true. It made absolute sense to me, especially with my promise to that Spirit that came to me. Since that Spirit (baby) came to me, my life changed. Once I moved to Nanaimo for school, there was no turning back.

Over those two years, with all the help, I was able to forgive myself. Holy, I thought I was going to take my guilt to the grave! I never thought it would be possible to forgive myself.

I learned many things about myself during that time. I learned that I had a gift, many gifts. And I would use them to help others. Different healers and seers told me that I would help many people. I would help at first by using my hands, then after some time I would be able to heal without even touching people. I'd be able to heal with my mind.

I was told that all I have to do is show up, and it will all happen. I was told I can interpret dreams. I was told I needed to weave. When I weave, I have patterns that are mine, that I wove in other lifetimes and are different from others. At the time, I was still young, so I didn't take these messages very seriously. The predictions felt so far away from me. They were big, and I felt so unworthy and insignificant. Plus, it was all a little scary! It felt like such a huge burden and responsibility. At fifty-five, I understand. I know now what I was told and what they meant.

Completing the Cycle

The Spirit had come and gone, leaving me with a gift—the promise that I would change my life, do good in the world. My original due date for the baby would have been December 11. Four years later, to the day, I woke up early one morning to go to the bathroom. When I got up out of bed, I immediately felt sore in my vaginal area. I sat down to pee and it stung, just like after giving birth. I remember how much it stung and how long that first pee is after giving birth; it goes on and on and on now that your bladder isn't pressed on. It was painful! I had no idea what was going on. I sat in the bathroom in the dark, with the laundry room light on across the hall, questioning things. *Did I get an STD? What the hell is going on?!* After a few minutes, the memory of the baby came strong! I suddenly knew that my body was completing the process of the birth that had been interrupted.

A few months later, I went to see a seer to learn more about the December 11 experience. I didn't tell her about the abortion, but somehow she could intuit it. She told me that my body didn't complete the birth process, it was interrupted by the abortion. Now that it had completed the process, my body released the memory from itself. It had taken four years to complete this cycle. Having this knowledge that the cycle was complete was a powerful thing. I knew that it had been part of something bigger, a plan between the spirit world and me. And now the pain and suffering, the guilt and the mourning, the verbal abuse from the dad—it was all done. Completing the birthing process gave me permission that I could let go; I could put a stop to hurting myself and stop the suffering. This freed my mind. I learned a lot from that experience, and I still do. It has helped me help others who have experienced this also.

Unexpected Medicine

Where I come from, you can't refer to your own self as a healer or seer because it's embarrassing. If you call yourself a healer then you aren't one, because healers don't say that about themselves. It's shameful to speak of yourself that way. Someone else can speak of you that way but not yourself. We are not allowed to boast of ourselves; that's for others to do. I would not call myself a healer, or a seer. I feel the people that possess those skills are far more advanced.

I heard stories from my aunty, who is recently deceased, who told me that way back her uncle was sick; he had something wrong with his head. The healer told him to go to the river at dawn. Told him what and who he needed to bring with him. When they got to the river, the healer started doing the ceremony and then began working on the man, saying prayers, chants. In the process, he started sucking something from the man's head. When the healer went to blow the substance he had sucked out of the man's head into the river, it was blood. The river turned red from the blood the healer had sprayed into it. He continued to do this until he healed the man. The man was healed and never had issues after that. This is what a True Healer is to me! I am not one. But I will own that I am a helper! I am a servant. I work for the Creator. I work for my ancestors. I will say that I am a pretty good helper but not a healer.

My path to helping others has been quite the journey. Some days, though not as often anymore, I remember this all happened because of a promise I made to the Spirit, the Soul that came to help me by bringing me a gift! This promise to make a difference and help others was made before coming to Earth. It was what I was already going to do. The baby solidified it. After decades, I did it because unconsciously there was a promise. But it was just who I was … who

I am now. Knowing this, I now feel so blessed and so loved.

In the years that I have been impacting people with counselling and facilitating, I know there are many people who have been helped by my gift, and, in turn, they have reciprocated by helping me learn to value my gift.

Linda was a beautiful Soul who taught me about the medicine in alcohol and drugs. I had no idea that was even possible!

In our one-on-one session, during our fourth or fifth week together, she began sharing, and as she did so, I felt like I could see this movie play above her head. Up to that point, it was very rare for me to "see." Linda got very emotional describing how all the people in her life have let her down, have hurt her at one point or another, and how she couldn't really count on them. In the "movie," I could see that the drinking and drugging she was doing was helping her at that time. I was not sure I was correctly interpreting what I was being shown, as I had never seen this in anyone else before. Still, I watched and paid attention to what I was being shown while listening to her.

When she stopped talking, I asked, "Linda, what would've happened if you didn't have drugs and alcohol in those dark times?" She gasped, then her head dropped and she started sobbing. I was surprised. Her response was so quick and strong. I waited for her to move through her emotions. When she was done, she lifted her head up, looked at me with tears still falling as she nodded, acknowledging something to herself that she couldn't before. She said, "Shelley, alcohol and drugs are my best friends!" She said it so matter-of-factly. "If I didn't have drugs in those darkest times of my life, I would have never survived. I would have been dead a long time ago," she explained. "They are my best friends. They are the only ones I could count on. The only ones that would come through for me!" She was crying. I had tears falling also, I was so moved. We sat in silence for a while. When there was an opening, I validated her. I told her, "I was shown an image of exactly what you said, that's why I asked you that question." She still had slow tears falling.

After another opening presented itself, I said, "Linda, I have five best friends. These women have gotten me through my darkest times. I cannot imagine living without any of them, let alone getting rid of any of them! How are you going do this? How are you going to be able to live without your 'best friends'?" She said, "Shelley, I have grown out of my friends. Yes, they got me through the darkest times in my life, but I have outgrown them. They are no longer keeping me alive. They are killing me." We both had tears. I smiled and told her how amazing and insightful that was.

She said, "It's time for me to let them go. They have done me good, but I got things to do and a big life ahead of me. I will go to the beach and do a ceremony this weekend and let them go. I will release them back to the light." I asked if she needed help. She knew exactly what she needed to do and didn't need my assistance. She did the ceremony on the weekend and felt her life had been changed by it.

After this session I couldn't go back to thinking about alcohol the same way. A&D were her friends! They were her medicine! I absolutely felt the truth in what she said, and I began to view substances and people with addictions totally differently. In a way, I learned to have a kind of gratitude for these substances. It was like they were buying time until the people found their way back to the light. Like a grace period. I learned that substance can be a medicine: what the medicine looks like depends on how the person is using it, and that's what determines the outcome. Some people are able to find their way back from addictions on their own, while many others keep going and don't make the journey back without a helping hand, and unfortunately some don't make it out alive. I will never forget that beautiful woman and the gift she gave me. By coming to the program and helping herself, she allowed me to take the journey with her, and from those experiences, with all the people I have helped serve and from Spirit showing me how to help them, I was able to grow and heal as a witness. Doing this work has helped me become a better person at God speed.

Thank you Linda for your courage and for choosing life in its darkest times! The time with you was a gift to my growth in every direction. I am a better person and better helper because of you!

Walking Through It

When I think about the reciprocal benefits of working with my clients, I remember a particular client; I'll call him Dennis. He came to the centre I worked at to deal with specific issues caused by the Residential School he had attended. I was his counsellor. The treatment program was just short of six weeks, and we felt we didn't have much time to do the healing work he wanted, so we took inventory and made a fluid list and got right to it. After the third week, we did processes of him looking at himself as a little boy who felt like no matter what he did, parts of himself were stuck at the school and he could never be free from it. I asked him if he was ready. He said, "Ready for what?" I said, "To go over to the RS site." The building itself had been demolished and its materials shipped out, but we could go on the grounds where it once stood. He agreed—he was ready. We went to the site, and he walked me through the parts of the school as they existed in his memory. He shared the horrible things that had happened to him and had been done to others. It was hard to hear, and I was grateful to hold space and be the container for him to pour into.

He started sharing stories of the times the kids paid back the nuns and priests for all their abuse and got away with it. How they stole food for the starving kids, and many other things. What touched me was that the pain he still suffered from was due to not being able to always help the kids who were being hurt and going hungry. The kids who died there that he couldn't protect. With all that he had personally endured, the pain that kept him bound to the school was that of his friends, family, and others whom he couldn't help. This is the pain that haunted him! After he cried and I cried with him, he was able to tell the stories of the blessings and good that happened. When he got to laugh and smile and remember the good he got out of that place in spite of the brutality, it lifted my heart. He shared the victories with a sweet giggle, a beautiful smile on his face, and light in his eyes.

After the laughs, he looked at me and said, "Thanks Sis! This really helped me." I said, "Oh no Bro, you did this! You're the one who faced all this pain and walked through it. A job well done! Thank you."

He looked at me. He said, "Look at me," in a stern voice. I was surprised. I looked at him. He was crying. He said, "Shelley. I have been to many treatment centres, all kinds of programs to heal this up. None of them have done what you did for me here today!" Now I started crying. He said "Sis, you did this! You helped me heal today! You helped me release all those kids that haunted me. I can't thank you enough! Thank you!" By this time, he had his big strong arm around me. My arm was around his waist. He pulled me closer, and I tightened my grip too. I said, "You're welcome! And thank you; I am so glad I was able to help!" We both smiled tearily as he said, "More than you will ever know Sis!" We nodded yes to each other and started walking back to the centre.

That day, I was able to help him set those kids free, even if only from his mind. I still feel blessed when I think of the work he did, if all I did was listen to him share how he helped them and how he wasn't able to help them. That day, I gave him the space to remember them and tell them they could go home, to tell them that he remembered them and they were free now and so was he. If all I did was witness, I was more than happy to do that for him.

I totally see Dennis in a whole new light. I have such a new respect for this beautiful man. Such a selfless soul.

Reflections and Gratitude

It has now been thirty years—to the day—since having the abortion. Looking out to the water off the patio at the Casa de Influencia, I sit and reflect on all that has happened since this tragic blessing!

In the first decade, I spent most of my time learning about how I was going be a helper. Spirit pushed and pulled me to this training, to that workshop, to that healer, to this seer. They were building my capacity for how I was going to teach and help others.

I quickly learned that I was serving something. This space, place, connection was *way bigger than me* in the greatest way possible. Somewhere on the journey, I found my connection to that force. I used to feel despair and loneliness as a child, but after finding that deep, sacred connection to a higher source, I haven't been alone since. I do have pain, but it isn't the deep and dark abyss the way it used to be before this connection.

The Creator, Ancestors, the Gods, the Supernatural Beings bring who comes forward when needed. When I am called on for help, whether the issue is big or small, I am never alone. I know now that the Creator sends people to me for assistance and I am sent to others for assistance. Always I give and receive. I used to get scared to help in the beginning, but after all these years, I have learned that it is Spirit that brings people to me, or me to them. So, anything the person needs, Spirit will provide.

I pray each morning for assistance, for guidance. I first pray for the day as I want it to be, and then for Spirit to show me what's needed for the day. This sounds simple, but it has taken me thirty years of searching and serving to get good at what I do. No matter how hard, it has always been rewarding and worth it.

As I sit here on the patio, I realize that, until I woke up this morning, I had never thought about what could have happened if I didn't abort the baby. I am in an insightful place, and for a few moments I felt this overwhelm of grief. Through many different moments and experiences, the dad and I believed that the baby was a girl. I know the agreement was that the Spirit would plant the gift and then return back to the spirit world. But how would it have played out if I had chosen to keep her? She would have had to die, but when? Would she have died in the next trimester, or at birth? She would have gone back because that's how it works; it was what was agreed. I cry, imagining the pain of that!

I cry because I imagine the pain that would have been for me, the boys, and the dad. The dad and I never spoke of how devastating it would have been for our sons if I had kept the baby and the boys knew they were having a brother or sister, only for it to die. That would have blown our family to pieces!

I cry because I have never seen this part, this version of the possible outcome, before this moment. I cry because me aborting the baby, giving it back to Spirit, was the best-case scenario. My suffering was an act of mercy for my sons.

I cry because my mind is releasing these last bits of pain and guilt through my body as I write. Gradually, I have been able to shift my outlook from it being the hardest, most awful thing "I did" to my greatest gift. I am not proud, but I do accept it, and now that I understand the spiritual part of what happened, I am able to live with myself.

I can see how this is the last part of the agreement, the last part of the promise I made to the baby! As I sit here in Puerto Vallarta to write my chapter for this book, the true purpose is to get to this "point of impact," to let it go, to release it, to heal the wound, and to restore myself in a way that feels more like a reconfiguring of my whole life, especially my relationship with the dad and my relationship with my children! From this I know I am free from my promise! The promise made was from the depth of despair, and it was motivating me negatively.

True, it was the promise that put me on a path to serving others. Through thirty years of keeping my promise, I have been able to help so many people. In session rooms, retreats, workshops, ocean cleansing ceremonies, on buses, airplanes, in the meat aisle at my grocery store, I have helped people. I am only saying that I have many experiences of helping people in many expected and unexpected places. I know this because they have told me so! They have told me and thanked me for what I did to help them. When I first began using my gift in this way, I would not really pay attention to the thanks, because I wouldn't allow myself to receive anything good from keeping my promise. Every time someone thanked me, it only validated the promise! Every time I left after making a difference, it proved that I was keeping my word to the promise! I wasn't able to absorb it. I didn't feel worthy.

From serving others I started to learn about myself. Only then could I heal and restore myself to my highest self, and thus begin to love myself. The more I loved myself, the more love I could receive. We have all heard that you can't love anyone until you love yourself. I never believed that. I'd always have a few cuss words in my mind when I'd hear this! I felt I was always good at loving and caring for others—in fact, I was told I loved largely. I could love big. But, I couldn't receive love! If you don't love yourself, you won't let yourself receive the love from others! Over time, I realized that the more I loved myself and received love, the more connected I got to Creator, the pure source! And the gift that was given to me grew stronger and stronger.

Because of my mission to "make right" and "keep my promises," I went hard, and it cost the dad, and sadly, it cost my sons hugely. I can't make it different for them. I wish I could. In my own way, I have tried to make it up to them. So far, travel has been the greatest gift I could give them. I felt it was the best way to give my sons the experience of family and the best way to give of myself and be more for and to them.

This week is thirty years of making that promise, and now that I have become aware of the truth of it, I no longer have to do my work from a place of self-sacrifice. I am free from continually punishing myself, hurting myself, stretching myself thin, helping at all costs. In this moment, I feel this infinite connection and love! I feel no grief or hurt in any form! From here, I can serve others in a way that doesn't cost me or my family anything anymore. I am free to serve cleanly. I can do this work using my gift in true love, light, and peace which would be in harmony!

To all my sons, I didn't know better then. Without guidance, I did what I had to to be able to live with myself for the choice I made. The choice was to give you the best of what I could. The only thing I can do is ask for forgiveness.

To the dad, my prayer is that you can forgive yourself and you can forgive me. I believe we can still have that blessed life we promised each other with our kids and grandkids. Know that you are loved. Know that you have been one of my greatest teachers. You do and you will have that place in my heart. Thank you.

To all those of you who trusted me to help you, thank you for helping me keep my promise and awaken the gift and allow me to receive and heal myself as you were healing yourself!

To Shelley, what a great and amazing woman you have grown into. You're not perfect, and I love that about you. You are in no way close to perfect, because you are so much more than that! Shelley, I am here to remind you, you are "Whole & Holy." Gilakas'la!

To all my Spirit Friends, Guides, and Angels, thank you for teaching me so gracefully. I know I'm a handful and at times easily distracted—sorry for that. I smile and giggle at that, knowing I can be a huge pain in the ass. I know without a doubt that you love me fiercely! I know because of how I trust you! I know that anything is possible and to expect miracles! I can only do these things because of how you have walked with me in this life. I am continuously becoming the best version of myself because of you. Gilakas'la!

About Shelley J. Cook

Shelley J. Cook has been working in the healing field since she was twenty-six. She is First Nations and brings into her work the cultural and Traditional Knowledge she was born into. Shelley has travelled around the world and visited many places to first heal herself and then to serve those who she can in the highest way. As a counsellor and facilitator, she worked in a treatment centre for several years. Shelley has also worked in classrooms as an education assistant and a counsellor for high-risk youth. She is passionate about working with young people and wants to equip them with the resources that will help keep them on a good path. She loves this work because she says she can't stay the same—through the growth of others, there is always space in the movement forward to grow with them. Shelley knows that she is blessed by the reciprocity that is exchanged when sharing sacred space with another person. She is always in awe of the magic that happens when witnessing other people journey inward, find the hidden darkness, let it go, and choose the path of love.

www.facebook.com/shelley.j.cook
shelleyjanecook@gmail.com

7

Sculpting the Oak Tree: My Journey from Self-Betrayal to Self-Compassion

By Dr. Madeleine De Little

How would your life be different if …
You approached all relationships with
authenticity and honesty?
Let today be the day … You dedicate yourself
to building relationships on the solid
foundation of truth and authenticity.

— Steve Maraboli

Sculpting the Oak Tree: My Journey from Self-Betrayal to Self-Compassion

By Dr. Madeleine De Little

As therapists, we cannot ask our clients to reveal their vulnerable parts if we are not willing to explore our own vulnerabilities. So here I am, sharing my personal story of how working with Indigenous survivors of intergenerational trauma helped me confront my own shame and practice self-forgiveness around my use of alcohol.

I am a white settler, cisgender, privileged older woman. I have been married, separated, and widowed to one man, the father of our three beautiful adult daughters. I am finally now in a loving, cherishing relationship with a friend I have known for many years. I come from a middle-class, hard-working family and was brought up in England in the shadows of the Second World War. I don't see myself as having experienced trauma, but I know now that our conscious memories don't always hold on to trauma, and therefore I attempt to be mindful of what my body is telling me. I also now know I had probably laid down some negative beliefs about myself in my nervous system that would continue to operate unconsciously and somatically in the present.

Making and Breaking My Vow

My story begins with the impact of my father's alcoholism on our family, particularly on my mother. As a young child I watched my mother's loneliness, saw the food that had been left to keep warm in the oven being thrown out the next day. I heard the arguments. I remember how I could feel her sadness and how I "learned" to look after her when my father didn't come home. I would make her cups of tea; I would be a good girl and not create more work for her. I cleaned the house and helped with everything she wanted me to do. I became a professional pleaser. I also "learned" the family rule, which was to not talk about my father's absence, his alcoholism, his gambling, and his womanizing. Instead, I learned to listen to my mother and watch every subtle nonverbal communication within the family. I now understand that my father's habits were essential to his coping with his past traumas, but for the rest of the family they created a huge abyss of silence which was never addressed. He never drank at home, although there were plenty of bottles that he had "acquired" from his work as a customs officer at a local port. At about eighteen years old, when I was legally allowed to drink alcohol, I vowed to myself that I would not partake of it in any way. I promised myself that it would be for the rest of my life. My family had been devastated by alcohol—I would not repeat the pattern.

For some years I was able to stay committed to my vow. Yet, by the time I was in my early twenties, I had found love but at a cost. My partner was a social drinker, and over the next three years I succumbed to drinking to be with him. It was also an unspoken social expectation among the company we kept. We had a fun time as we pub-crawled our way through eleven pubs in one small English village. It felt good to have the social approval of my partner and his friends. Still, there was always a part of me that was ashamed that I had been weak and yielded to temptation. After three years we separated, but I had already forgotten my vow to myself. Drinking alcohol daily in the pub (although not to excess) became a normal, acceptable, social behaviour for me. I had also started to smoke. I had met some French men through my work, and they smoked Gauloises. I loved the smell and could not resist a puff or two. Then another, and another, until I was buying packs for myself.

At thirty years old I moved from England to Canada to see if I could make a go of marrying a charming, intelligent, funny, dear Canadian man that I had met on a Greek beach. I stopped smoking the day I got on the plane, but the glass of wine or two still flowed, and I later discovered that I had chosen a drinker for a life partner.

I found work as a teacher in British Columbia. One of my mentors who was training me in the Bowen Family Systems Theory of counselling saw the potential in me and suggested that I become a counsellor. So that's what I did. I started my training, and before completing my degree I was already working in a high school as a school counsellor. From working with many students, I soon learned how subtle this work is and how it is a two-way process: Whatever I had lingering in every cell of my body would make itself known to me and possibly the world at some point. My subsequent training in the Satir Model highlighted this somatic message to me with its focus on the importance of internal bodily sensations. From this training I felt confident I could make counselling experiential by accessing the shifting sensations in the body of the client. At one point in my Satir Model training, one of the assignments was to write a forgiveness letter around a personal situation that was calling for closure. I chose to write to my father, and I actually put on an international stamp and posted it to him. Nothing. Silence. No response. In retrospect I was not surprised, as he had never written to me before.

Years later, on the eve of his funeral, my mother tossed a tattered envelope to me and said, "Here, this is for you.... Your dad never wrote me anything."

It was a handwritten letter. In it, he explained and apologized for his behaviour, blaming his drinking on the war and all that he had seen and done. I found it in me to forgive him posthumously, but to this day I wonder if he had passed his trauma down to me genetically.

By that time, my husband and I had brought the first two of my three little girls into the world, and I was now fully aware that the man I had married and loved had a serious mental illness that he coped with by using excessive amounts of alcohol, among other substances. How history repeats itself! At first I would join him occasionally, and then it became every night at dinner. My nightly drinking habit continued even into my next (and current) loving relationship, ignoring my teenage commitment to myself. I say "ignoring," but that's not absolutely true. The vow I made was always there, but I was able to subconsciously justify my drinking, argue with myself, and rationalize it.

Success, Sand Trays, and Imposter Syndrome

Despite my drinking, I achieved many successes in my work as a counsellor. Over the course of a number of years, I developed a therapeutic model called Neuroscience and Satir in the Sand Tray (NSST). NSST is somatic work that functions in many ways, two of which are most relevant here: Clients use figurines that act as portals to their bodies, and then, through somatic countertransference, the therapist's body picks up the sensations in the client's body. In this way, some of the impacts of the past trauma on the client's body are welcomed by the therapist into their own body as an ongoing diagnostic tool. Notably, this process also awakens past implicit unconscious memories in the therapist.

NSST is a paradigm shift in the modern psychotherapeutic world as it enables clients to access their stored bodily memories through imagination, play, and creativity. Because the left side of the brain, which controls logic and speech, is not directly connected to the body, basic talk therapy will not release the sequestered images of past trauma held somatically, that is, in the body itself. So, we have to figure out how to get to and transform these protected parts that reside in the body in a way that is not through the logical language of the left brain but rather through the metaphorical, image-based language of the right brain.

The past traumatic experiences of abuse and neglect are stored in the unconscious catacombs of our memories in the form of images. These stored experiences are not available to the conscious mind nor are the ways that our nervous system has automatically protected us from them. These protective defences of the autonomic system (commonly known as "fight, flight, freeze, and collapse") exist on a continuum of healthy to unhealthy defences that impact us mentally and often physically. They were needed at the time of the traumatic event(s), but over time they become problematic for us. The work in the sand tray is to bring these protective ways of coping out into the light through the use of the figurines.

My counselling office is filled with figurines and a sand tray, and in the NSST therapy sessions it is some of these figurines that reso-nate with the stored past traumatic experiences. Through the act of creating scenes in the sand tray, we enable the figurines to become projections of our internal world in time and space. Once a client's past default ways of coping are on display in the sand tray, the client can experience them consciously and decide if they wish to maintain them. This shift in awareness allows for dormant and unexpressed genetic material to create new neural pathways that, in turn, create a new sense of being. In other words, by creating new connections between a person's body and brain, they can create a new sense of self. This new image of self is then internalized and literally changes the structure of the brain and the nervous and hormonal systems forever. For the client, this work is deep and lasting, as evidenced by anecdotal reports from hundreds of my clients.

Upon seeing how effective NSST was for my clients in Canada, I decided to share this method internationally. I began travelling around the world, teaching the NSST method. But everywhere I went, negative thinking started to implode within me while I taught: *If they only knew me, really knew me, they would know that I had broken my vow, that I am not being authentic with myself, that I am not doing anything special.* More and more, I felt like an imposter.

Still, my counselling business became very successful. I wrote my book, entitled *Where Words Can't Reach: Neuroscience and the Satir Model in the Sand Tray*, and then went back to university to complete a PhD in Education, studying the impact of teaching this method to student therapists. I began to be invited to teach in various countries and speak at conferences, and many clients came to me through word of mouth. Did these things change my sense of being an imposter? Nope! There were two parts of me continually arguing about not being good enough and yet excited and determined to be the best I could be. If anything, the former fuelled the latter. The drink before and after dinner helped settle my excited-anxious, wired-tired, false sense of self that I had inadvertently laid down in my nervous system.

Intergenerational Trauma

Since Covid, I decided to work mostly with adult clients with early relational trauma and intergenerational trauma, as NSST is one of the few therapeutic interventions that can transform such trauma. We now know that the past experiences of our family members are epigenetically passed down to us through our genes, and even though these inherited experiences are unknown to us, they have the potential to negatively impact our lives. People are not consciously aware of how their bodies respond to the trauma encoded in their DNA, and yet their bodies cry out to find safety, love, and connection. For some, it means they use certain unconscious behaviours to help calm their nervous systems. At some point, those unconscious behaviours become problematic for them.

Specifically, I realized I was drawn more and more to working with some of my older clients who were dealing with deep, unconsciously held intergenerational trauma that could not be fully reached with words, and which often involved alcoholism. I started to work in the remote villages of northern Canada where many Indigenous people live. I would fly in via a seaplane for a week at a time and work ten hours a day to support the people in their communities. These beautiful souls of all ages had been harmed by European and Canadian colonization, the Indian Act, the Indian Residential School system, and the Sixties Scoop. Under the policies of the Canadian government, generations of Indigenous children were taken from their families and communities and placed in residential schools. Others were adopted into primarily white families to assimilate them and strip them of their cultures. In both instances, the children frequently endured physical, sexual, and emotional abuse from the priests, nuns, and teachers in the schools and from their adoptive families. Whilst I was aware of the history of Indigenous Peoples in Canada, I was not prepared for how it is being manifested today. The legacy of so much trauma and the impact of ongoing racism and lack of support and understanding was shocking for me. Indigenous Peoples do have their own ways of healing, but racism and oppression has made it difficult for people to access them. Many of them have coped with the impact of these epigenetically transferred traumas by excessive alcohol use and, for some, abusing their loved ones in all the ways imaginable. The name for this is "lateral abuse." The alcohol use would last, in some cases, for days, and the child neglect and domestic violence were rampant. One of my First Nations colleagues described this child neglect as "multi-generational abandonment."

Trauma is about perceiving oneself as trapped and alone. The trauma, lateral abuse, and multi-generational abandonment in these communities has left many members with a sense of hopelessness and a felt sense of something not "working" for them. The emotional legacy of colonization is trapped energetically inside every cell of their bodies but is unable to be released. So, to try to regulate these unrestrained, irretrievable feelings, they use a temporary fix with substances like alcohol and drugs.

NSST in Practice

My method of counselling does not need the story of what has happened to those who come to see me. However, some people need for me to hear their story of past abuse and neglect. I respect that. Once the story has been told, I move them into their embodied right brain by having them use the figurines in the sand to try to show me the impact of their experience. They choose figurines (or more accurately, the figurines choose them energetically) depicting loneliness, entrapment, fear, and hopelessness.

I want to describe a session with one courageous woman. What follows is primarily based on this one person, but to keep her identity private, as the communities are so small, I have changed some of the details. This woman began by telling me the story of her chaotic life—her own multi-day binge drinking, sexual abuse by male relatives, not being able to work, and neglecting her five children, three of whom had different fathers. When ready to move to the sand tray, I invited her to practice by "selecting" a figurine, placing it in the tray and simply describing it. She picked one "at random"—I use quotation marks because the figurines are never truly chosen at random. The energy of the past experiences literally pulls the figurines off the shelves and into the client's hands. She "chose" a tiny mouse and placed it in the sand tray. As part of the NSST process, I described it to her to ensure that I was seeing the figurine and its placement in the same way as her. As I spoke, I had a sense of suffocation in my chest and a shrinking in my whole body. She then described the mouse as white, small, and scared. I asked her if her body was affected by this figurine, and she described how she could not breathe and wanted to hide away so that nobody would see her. I reassured her that we could stop whenever she needed to and that we could create a safe place in the sand tray for her to return to at any time.

Through my training and many years of experience, I have developed an intuitive, empathic connection to my clients that is expressed somatically both in the client and myself. While in this place of deep connection, I was able to sense that my client's breathing was shallow, her body posture was slumped, her voice was quiet, and the tone of her facial muscles was soft. These non-verbal cues of her body suggested strongly that she was in a state of near-collapse which occurs when the body is terrified (like a rat in a cat's mouth). Her nervous system had needed to collapse in order to survive her genetically inherited and lived trauma. To use neuroscientific terms, she was in a parasympathetic collapse known as a "dorsal vagal" or "immobilized" state.

I invited her to place her hands in the sand tray and cross them over slowly. This bilateral exercise crosses the midline of the body and allows the two hemispheres of the brain to connect, which then activates the lower part of the brain. I have found that this kinesthetic activity also allows the body to release any tension. This is exactly what happened to my client. As I watched her, I immediately felt the suffocation easing in my chest, which is most likely what she was experiencing as well. I allowed her to take her time and notice if her breathing was becoming deeper in her chest. This activity allowed both of her hemispheres to connect and then begin to regulate her nervous system. In neuroscientific terms, the ventral branch of the vagus nerve was activated, which in turn brought her out of her collapsed state and put a brake on her dorsal vagal nerve.

During all of this, I was connecting deeply with her through the attachment mechanism of both our right hemispheres. This right-brain-to-right-brain communication was beyond the words of her story of what happened to her in the past. I was helping my client find deeply stored unconscious memories, bring them out into the tray through the figurines, and explore them consciously. It is a two-way process. I am with my client experiencing their pain. I am always prepared for this and know how to regulate and take care of myself.

But this time, the process was shedding light on an implicit, deeply stored, hitherto unconscious memory of my own. As I viewed her sand tray, I experienced in my body a profound "aha!" moment. I can only describe it like a lightning bolt striking me as I felt sick to my stomach, remembering my vow. For the first time in my adult life, I saw, consciously in my mind's eye, a picture of myself as a teenager making a vow to never drink.

As my client and I connected in this way through the metaphor of her figurines, she could begin to feel deeply seen and heard, like a child sensing the safety of their mother. She could experience a new physical freeing and lightness of being that contrast to the traumatic experience of being trapped and alone. A glimpse of what it would be like to be safe. To reinforce this experience for her, I invited her to create a small scene of a time when she felt safe. This ventral brake provided a safety net that she could return to at any time, as it was able to at least temporarily shut off the collapse survival mechanism that her body had to develop in order to live. In this scenario, she placed a small child on a swing being pushed by an older adult male. She added some flowers and a small dog. As she placed this image of safety and peacefulness in the sand tray, I noticed my chest becoming less tight—my nervous system was reacting to her picture. She said she was experiencing a much lighter sensation in her body, and she smiled as she described the picture as being fun, free, and safe. Now she was ready to work on the impact of the past in the sand tray.

I invited her to show me how she was experiencing herself on that day, in the present. She was drawn to and placed in the sand tray a figurine of a solitary woman. She put the woman figurine in a cave with her head bent, facing a huge three-headed dragon. Simply and without adjectives, I described to her how I saw the scenario she made: "I see a woman in a cave, and she has her head bent down …" As I said this, I felt a slight trembling in my body and my chest felt constricted. My body was picking up on her physical sensations. Without telling her story of what happened in the past, my client described the picture she had made using the figurines in the sand. She said, "The woman feels ashamed, and trapped in the cave because there is a dragon outside waiting to consume her if she leaves." She said that the cave provided safety.

I looked at the sand tray again and noticed that she had tucked a miniature bottle of alcohol into the back of the cave. I chose not to comment on it at that time; however, I intuited her full awareness of its presence. Instead, I asked how her body was responding to the whole picture. She placed her hand on her chest and described how she could barely breathe.

Through the metaphors of the figurines in the sand tray, we explored how she would like to be different. She created another scenario using different figurines. This time, there was a large oak tree, a hummingbird, and a sign that said "peace." She then pushed the sand away from the middle of the tray to reveal the blue-painted base, into which she placed some whales. She brought the original swing with the flowers from her safe place into this picture to show how she would like to be different.

In response to these images, which the Satir Model calls "yearnings," I felt my chest relax and expand with a sense of power and lightness. My client similarly said that, after assembling this scene, she was able to breathe more deeply and her shoulders were more relaxed. To continue to explore the shift in her bodily sensations, I had her sculpt the two different scenarios using her own body. I invited her to stand up with me, and together we sculpted the same position as the woman with her head down. Then we changed position and both moved into being the strong oak tree. This time her head was up, she was looking around, and she said her feet felt grounded like the roots of the oak tree.

By sculpting the oak tree, her body was also able to experience a new way of being. This new way of being came about because the experience had shifted her nervous system the same way as the picture of her past safe place had previously done. This time though, it was grounded in the belief that it would be a more permanent way of being. By using the figurines in this way, her nervous system would become more and more in a ventral vagal state referred to as a congruent state of peace, and it would change her sense of self in the present. I also experienced a shift in my own body as I took on the position of the oak tree. It was a profound moment of awareness of the potential to be strong and grounded and clear about what I wanted for myself.

Through this positive and powerful experience, my client's genetic expression through epigenetics was changing the actual physiology of her survival mechanism from a collapsed state to a playful state, also known as the ventral vagal state. She was still the same person, but she would experience more safety in herself and with others. She described in words how she would be different now and that she would make amends with her past and present behaviours. We continued to work together, and in subsequent sessions her individual therapy developed into how to help other community members. Other clients I saw there also experienced similar epiphanies, and I was delighted to see how NSST could change people's lives so quickly and profoundly.

Holding My Own Head Up

Despite these clear gains, there was a palpable somatic discomfort inside of me. The pain for me was that I was not being authentic with them, as I also drank alcohol. Although I was not addicted to alcohol in the way that many of the community members were, I had taken a vow not to drink and I had broken that vow. Even though the vow was only for myself, I had broken it.

I had heard story after story of how alcohol had harmed so many community members so profoundly. How could I sit with these people and feel my own shame around alcohol? My body was filled with anxiety that they would find out my lack of authenticity and refuse to see me. This sense of my own self-betrayal was becoming louder in my head and body, and I knew I had to do something. Still, it took me a long time to seek out support.

A year ago, when I was teaching abroad, I had significant pain in my stomach, and I sought care from my regular family doctor when I returned to Canada. She was not particularly helpful, so I decided to try alternative medicine to explore the underlying causes of my stomach pain. I went to a naturopath who helped me with my gastro-systemic problem and said I should not drink, as alcohol is a carcinogen (I am a cancer survivor). She invited me to try to do a "dry January" and I agreed. With a handful of natural remedies, I went away to heal my body and my sense of betrayal of myself. I was able to stick to my decision to not drink for January, and then February came, and I just carried on enjoying mocktails and non-alcoholic drinks. I said no to offers of wine, and I continue to be able to do so at this time of writing. I felt and continue to feel free of the betrayal.

Now when I return to the remote northern communities, I can hold my head up. I look my clients in their eyes and allow people to look at me, knowing I have nothing to hide. I no longer have a stain on my soul. I don't tell them my story, but the energy when I am with them is different. It is uncluttered with negative self-talk about being an imposter. I also know a little more about the struggle faced by people with addictions, and I have found more compassion for those who need alcohol to numb the pain of a trauma that has no words. I can now be true to myself, and I am grateful for the opportunity to reflect on my vulnerability and my journey through shame and toward authenticity.

As I said in the beginning of this chapter, we can't ask our clients to be vulnerable if we are not willing to go there ourselves. Because I have been able to transform my own vulnerability, I feel more genuine and comfortable facilitating other people's journeys into their hidden vulnerable parts and helping them to transform them.

About Dr. Madeleine De Little

Dr. Madeleine De Little, PhD, CCC, MTC, RCS, is a leading world expert on and the creator of the Neuroscience and Satir in the Sand Tray (NSST) method of transforming intergenerational trauma. With over forty years of counselling experience, she has recently been called to work with Indigenous survivors of intergenerational trauma in remote communities in northern Canada, where the impact of generations of profound harm is manifest in lateral violence, neglect, sexual abuse, and alcoholism. Dr. De Little is the recipient of the 2021/2022 Canadian Counselling and Psychotherapy Association's Counsellor Practitioner Award. She is also the Research Chair of the Satir Institute of the Pacific and a senior faculty member of the Banmen Satir China Management Center. Dr. De Little is the author of *Where Words Can't Reach: Neuroscience and the Satir Model in the Sand Tray*, and she teaches the NSST method and supervises student counsellors around the world.

wherewordscannotreach.ca
www.facebook.com/madeleine.d.little/

8

The Time of the Lone Wolf Is Over

By Dr. Rick Miners

We get together on the basis of our similarities;
we grow on the basis of our differences.

– Virginia Satir

The Time of the Lone Wolf Is Over

By Dr. Rick Miners

As I begin, I wish to express my appreciation to the Musqueam, Squamish, and Tsleil-Waututh peoples on whose unceded ancestral territories I have lived for more than fifteen years, and to the Indigenous individuals I have had the honour and privilege to work, dance, sing, and laugh with.

* * *

Did Dyani just call me a "beautiful Indian man"?! I was beyond elated. I was finally being seen. She and I were sitting in a circle of Indigenous leaders, Elders, and chiefs, debriefing yesterday's plant medicine ceremony. It was late morning, and we had settled back into the same space as yesterday's ceremony: a rustic hall in a retreat centre nestled among ancient cedars alongside a meandering stream. During the ceremony, Dyani had journeyed so very far, out to the feathered edges of her consciousness. In those moments, only she knew what she was experiencing … and some of us were getting worried. Had she gone irretrievably far? Would she be able to come back? As concern mounted, others casually approached, sat beside her, and tried to guide her at least part way back to consensual reality. Dyani would have none of it. She seemed to be revelling in her experience, and she wanted to stay right where she was. I settled in nearby, sensing she might need a witness, a companion presence, to tether her to this realm but also to safely support her as she soared wherever she needed without interference.

As others stepped away, space became available to sit in front of her. I did so gingerly, not wanting to disrupt the flow of her experience. Eventually, Dyani signalled that she wanted to clasp hands, like we were going to arm wrestle. At some point, her other hand joined the clasp, so she was gripping my thumb with both of her hands. Sensing her physical strength, concerns about the wellbeing of my thumb momentary flitted through my head. Yet I set them aside, determined to remain present and meet Dyani with loving awareness wherever she was. We spent what seemed like long moments gazing deeply into each other's eyes. It was like we were meeting in another realm, like two waves on the ocean simultaneously recognizing each other and realizing that we sprang from the same source. My intuition in that moment suggested this was the case, but I hadn't known for sure until she shared the next day.

My ancestry is European through and through, yet I have long felt an inexplicable calling to Indigenous ways. Some of my distant ancestors crossed the Atlantic as long ago as the 1660s, yet more immediate relatives sought out a better life here in Canada as recently as the 1920s. Primarily of Anglo-Saxon Protestant descent, they hailed mostly from today's England, yet also from other countries in northwestern Europe. While tracking my ancestry through time, I discovered that my Indigenous roots are most likely Celtic. With that said, when I was a pre-teen and aware of only the most recent generations of my ancestry, Aboriginal peoples from Australia rocked my world during a televised opening ceremony of an international sporting event. Dressed in full regalia, they danced and sang in fierce and beautiful unison. It was unlike anything I'd ever seen. Without a hint as to why, I was captivated.

My childhood contained many happy moments. My family was involved in the community: we knew neighbours, played sports, hosted celebrations, went camping and to relatives' cottages, and travelled internationally. Religion was divisive in my family, so my exposure to it was minimal and troubling. In a nutshell, my physical and intellectual needs were met, but my emotional and spiritual education were incomplete. Combined with shame from an early childhood event, frequent family moves, and sometimes counterintuitive rules, I grew up experiencing a vague sense of unease that, in retrospect, was due to disconnection from my intuition and spirituality. So, the performance of the Aboriginal peoples during the opening ceremony struck me like a lightning bolt, piercing the carapace of my disconnection. Still, as time went by, I came to dismiss it as just a fanciful TV show with no bearing on reality or my life.

By young adulthood, however, a longing to explore existential questions arose. I travelled overseas, read ancient texts and recent philosophy, and looked into Christianity, Buddhism, Shamanism, and Indigenous ways of being and relating in the world. Some of these were familiar, yet didn't resonate. In the end, though I couldn't (and still can't) rationally explain their appeal, Indigenous ways, above all others, resonated in a way that felt like a homecoming. There was something about how they hold the natural world with awe and reverence. Regalia—emblazoned with animals, plants, or celestial bodies—burst with vitality and invoked mystery.

Ceremonies were animated by driving drum rhythms, exhilarating harmonies, ululation, and guttural roars. Behind the scenes was a hive of activity: people tending to the sacred fire, whipping up mass meals, or running errands—with everyone playing their part. The most awe-inspiring, though, were the Sundancers. They underwent grueling austerities and ceremonies with dignity and ardent devotion. I later learned of their almost constant prayers, which were mainly on behalf of the people. Initially, this all alarmed and overwhelmed me. Then it seized me. As I continued to attend Sundance and participate in ceremonies, I experienced a sense of non-dual oneness, of immediacy, with the elements of the natural world, as if I and it were all made of the same stuff, as if the boundaries that delimit "me" and "other" temporarily fell away. I sensed a connection, a belonging, to something tangible and vast. Here was a dirt-under-your-fingernails spirituality.

* * *

As a therapist, I feel it is important to acknowledge what an honour and privilege it is to be present with clients as they engage in the intimate, transformative work of therapy. I have learned something from many clients about myself, humanity, and the human condition. Every so often, a client or group of clients I have assisted have indelibly impacted my life. One such group was the group of Indigenous leaders, Elders, and relations mentioned above who sought to heal from intergenerational trauma originating in Canada's Indian Residential School system.

This group's aim was to reprocess their trauma, learn therapeutic modalities that complement their ancestral practices, and then, with an eye to autonomy, teach this integrated approach to others in their nations and communities. This work took place in a ceremonial space that had been carefully prepared to invoke the sacred. Upon entering, everyone smudged and sat in a circle. Indigenous leaders opened with introductions, land acknowledgments, words of welcome, words that named historical wrongdoings, and ancestral spiritual teachings. Settler psychotherapists (I among them) then introduced ourselves and our approaches to therapy, highlighting similarities to Indigenous worldviews when possible. Participants introduced themselves and shared their intentions and challenges. Some participants consented to processing their challenges within the circle, while others did so later, working one-on-one with a leader or therapist. The next morning, participants smudged and settled on their cushions. Leaders honoured the participants' courage to do this important work to heal themselves, their ancestors, and their nations from historical harms. The therapists reviewed housekeeping, safety agreements, the likely arc of the journey, how to navigate challenging experiences, and how to request or decline support. Participants then revisited their intentions in silence and ingested their ancestral plant medicine. Hours later, once they had returned to ordinary awareness, a snack was served in an adjacent space. Some chatted or drew mandalas there. Others processed their experience further with a therapist, strolled the grounds, or retired to their rooms to journal or nap. After a communal supper, we had a group check-in and individual counselling was made available. The next morning, participants circled up in the ceremonial space where debriefing was facilitated by the therapists. As part of a closing ceremony that immediately followed the debriefing, Indigenous leaders shared ancestral teachings and songs and performed a gratitude ceremony to honour all therapists and staff who had supported at the retreat. This integrated approach drew upon complementary expertise and understandings from Indigenous and Western approaches to healing and was flexibly tailored to meet the arising needs of this group.

Much as I have some experience with Indigenous practices, witnessing profound changes arising from psychotherapy interwoven with Indigenous wisdom left a deep impression on me. Initially, group members had shown a variety of reactions to the presence of settler therapists like me: quiet wariness, fierce independence, cautious optimism, and good-natured welcome. Within hours of our first contact, their resilience, dignity, and determination to heal themselves and their peoples were apparent. Some spoke succinctly, yet with pride and affection, about their ancestral ways and languages. Some engaged minimally in the pleasantries that accompany getting acquainted, yet did engage in task-oriented, no-nonsense, or brief, unambiguous exchanges. Some spoke unflinchingly of the horrific impact of multi-generational harms perpetrated against Indigenous peoples by the Canadian government and others acting in its stead. In my eyes, their comments and demeanor conveyed the unmoving conviction that "you can't break us," and a simultaneous conditional invitation to support them as an ally. With this in mind, my therapeutic interventions were drawn primarily from Indigenous Focusing-Oriented Therapy for Complex Trauma (which weaves together mindfulness, land-based, and somatic elements), Satir Transformational Systemic Therapy, Cognitive Behavioural Therapy, and my experience with Indigenous cosmology and ceremonies.

As we became more acquainted and comfortable with each other, I came to feel at home there, connected to the land and curious about my ancestry, in a way I have rarely experienced in North America's mainstream culture. For example, early on the first morning of a retreat, I happened upon some of the men down at a nearby mist-shrouded stream, where we nodded in recognition not only of each other but also our shared activity: an invigorating splash in the chilly water. On a few other occasions, while taking in a spectacular view of grazing buffalo, a river, and snow-capped mountains beyond, I got to casually chat with a few participants about our lives, hobbies, and cultures. Once, when some participants used a sauna as a makeshift sweat lodge, I was invited to join them, and we drummed and sang a couple songs from the Sundance ceremony and chatted about common acquaintances and interests. I think we got most acquainted, though, while breaking bread during meals and during our formal sharing circles. Through these many shared moments, the participants' raw candour, thoughtful generosity, and ready humour touched me.

What impacted me most, however, was sitting beside, attuning to, and providing care to the participants—through smudging, holding a hand, whispering or making sounds of understanding, singing, or simply being present—as they gradually reprocessed multi-generational atrocities committed against their communities, devastating losses of loved ones, or repeated traumas to themselves. As the embers of something profound and achingly beautiful were gently fanned, resolute toughness began to give way to long-suppressed heartbreak, unspeakable shame became tolerable enough to begin to voice, and dark rage and abject terror started to lighten or dissipate. These shifts sometimes resulted in group members choosing healthier behaviours in their everyday lives, reaching out to others in their communities with more kindness, uplift, or hope, or showing up to subsequent retreats with more openness to connecting or more sparkle in their eyes. Witnessing these shifts in the lives of the participants altered my outlook by renewing my hope that humankind can bridge perceived differences and historical wrongdoings to trust and heal ourselves. It renewed my faith that spirit-infused psychotherapy can heal even such wounds as these, and it opened me to a rootedness, a more immediate sense of belonging, within a community.

* * *

"Thank you, Father," he said. Did I hear that right? Did Bill, an internationally respected Elder more than twenty years my senior, just call me "father"? I chalked it up to the mind-altering effects of the plant medicine and a temporary disconnect from consensual reality. However, the next day, when I was seated alone and enjoying the view, and when Bill was clearly in an ordinary state of mind, he approached me to share that he remembered thanking me. He explained that he had felt deeply moved during a song I had sung and that he had indeed experienced me as his father. The day before, he had been lying down not far from where I sat and had quietly sobbed with the voice of a little boy while I was singing an old Cree lullaby, which I had been granted permission to sing by a Cree Elder named Mechuskosis from the Michel Band in central Alberta. Whenever I sing that song and I'm able to "get out of my own way," it seems to me that something else is singing through me, like the presence of an ancient, caring, grandfatherly Indigenous man. Bill's sharing surprised and touched me—it seemed to confirm that I wasn't the only one who noticed the presence of something else working through me. It was as if I had served as a conduit, a medium, or, as some Indigenous Elders say, a "hollow bone" for an otherworldly presence to share its medicine through song.

This wasn't the first time I had felt this presence while singing. It first happened years earlier when I was in a sweat lodge at a Sundance ceremony in the mountains a few hours' drive from Vancouver, British Columbia. I had not ingested any plant medicines, but due to prayer and the rigours of dancing I had become more receptive to something much vaster, much greater than me, and as I surrendered to it, the way I sang changed. My jaw shifted slightly, my voice became more resonant and powerful, and the hairs on the back of my neck stood on end. It seemed like it was no longer me singing. I was initially alarmed, yet soon comforted by what seemed an ancient, benevolent, masculine Indigenous presence that was pleased to have found a way to access and share with the world again.

I, of course, had no way of knowing whether any of these imaginings were true. However, Joni, a self-described psychic who happened to be at Sundance, approached me some time later and shared an intuition: "In a former life, you were a Native American warrior who zigged when you should have zagged. You got hit and died." As suddenly as she had approached, she turned and walked away. I was speechless. Part of me longed to hear more because it somehow seemed so true; yet, as someone steeped in the scientific method, another part of me was anything but inclined to believe in past lives. Show me the evidence! I thanked her and inwardly dismissed the comment. Still, a seed had been planted.

With that said, when Indigenous people first asked me, a white settler, to sing Indigenous songs, it triggered fearful beliefs: *Who do you think you are to sing their songs?!* The last thing I would want is to be perceived as appropriating Indigenous Traditional Knowledge or culture. There is already a long, painful history of that (and so much more). However, while lending a hand with odd jobs or participating in ceremonies, I had somehow communicated my interest in learning, and permission to sing these songs was gifted to me with the understanding that I would honour their origins and share them in a good way. In the years since I was first invited to sing these songs and began to feel what is now a familiar felt sense of another being, I've been told the room goes silent when I sing, some people shed tears, and some are reminded of a loved one who has crossed over.

In moments like these, I'm honoured, humbled, and grateful that I heard about and was granted entry to the Sundance. It is one of the most profoundly moving community gatherings and spiritual practices I have ever encountered, and although I could not have known it then, it would prove to be a pivotal moment in my life. At

Sundance, people are drawn together through the common purpose of preparing the ceremonial space, grounds, and meals, through the play and laughter of children, and through funny or wise stories shared around evening campfires. In keeping with Sundance tradition, I helped with the sacred grandfather fire, sometimes through the night, for the first few years. Spending hours in nature, reverentially building and tending to a large fire and grandfather and grandmother stones, led to moments of reciprocity with the fire. It was as if this ancient element evoked an awareness of my challenges in life and then, through the dance of its flames, showed me an age-old solution. For some time thereafter, I would feel an inexplicable peace and sense of connection and belonging to the natural world. In the years after others took my place among the fire-keepers, I danced for several years and then, in subsequent years, I sang sacred songs and drummed with others on big drums.

Around the time I was first invited to experience and support dancers at Sundance, I developed an interest in plant medicines as a tool for healing. A respected Elder said, in a way that both dismissed my training in Western psychotherapy and piqued my interest, that taking a particular plant medicine was "like forty years of psychotherapy in a single session." What's more, he endorsed the belief held by some Amazonian shamans that Western psychology and psychiatry were like kindergarten in the psycho-spiritual world. By contrast, their shamanic approach was like "a PhD at the University of Universities." Intrigued, I read voraciously on the topic and sought out experience. I was fortunate to later work for a non-profit whose mission is to legalize MDMA-assisted psychotherapy to treat post-traumatic stress disorder. Previously, as a participant in their healthy volunteer study, I had taken MDMA and experienced first-hand the benefit of opening to a very young, shame-ridden, and vulnerable part of myself while in the abiding presence of two caring therapists for several hours. Later, I travelled to Brazil to experience ayahuasca in the experienced hands of Amazonian Indigenous healers. Ayahuasca is a psychoactive plant brew traditionally used in the Amazon. Among other effects, it induces temporary functional changes in the brain associated with vision, feelings, memories, and consciousness. It can amplify introspection and reprocessing of past and present stressors and may also engender powerful visions and strategies for a more hopeful future. Experiences such as these enhanced my sense of wellbeing, trust, and willingness to be truly seen by others; they accelerated the reprocessing of childhood wounds and intergenerational survival patterns; and they granted me glimpses into non-ordinary awareness and the loving awareness, the divine consciousness, at our core.

By this time, I had experienced vivid exchanges with plants that heightened my awareness of our reciprocal relationship with them and the natural world. These experiences further opened the matrix of my beliefs about what is possible. I came to appreciate that plants have a consciousness of their own and have much to teach us humans. For the record, much as plant medicines may, under the right circumstances, be an effective "power tool" in a therapist's toolbox and can accelerate or deepen healing in many clients, they are not for everyone. They are not a panacea, and it is debatable how many sessions of psychotherapy they might actually substitute for. More important than the plant ingested is the client's readiness, safety, intention, and mindset; the setting in which the healing occurs; and the preparation before and integration after what may prove to be among the most impactful experiences in a person's life.

* * *

After brief introductions all around, a man casually approached me and said, "Why are you here?" Somewhat taken aback by his directness and brevity, I replied, "To support." "What do you want?" he asked. I said, "To help in whatever way I can." He said, "Is that *really* what you want?" More taken aback by his directness and persistence, I hemmed and hawed momentarily, and as the wheels of my mind turned for an answer, I realized he was the leader. He continued, "What do you want?" I said, "To open my heart." Now smiling, he said, "Ah, there it is," and relented.

Through a series of synchronicities, which included volunteering to support the participants of a vision quest, I had found myself in a remote location northeast of Lillooet, British Columbia, at an Indigenous sweat lodge. Joe was the invited healer, though he would never refer to himself in this way; with humility, he described himself as someone with a few tools and some advice that people could choose to use or not. Joe circled away from me, engaged others, and then returned, saying, "Choose your poison." Getting somewhat used to his way of speaking, I went along with it and said, "What are the choices?" He pulled out two small metal containers and named the ointment in each. I made my choice and, with my consent, he applied dabs of the ointment to a few places on my body. Once he had completed this, I asked what the ointment was for. He indicated that in some places it was for healing, and, in others, for protection. I thanked him. Without missing a beat, Joe said, "Don't thank me. Thank the old man." Confused, I said, "What old man?" He said, "The one that's following you." Clearly not referring to the physical plane of existence, but rather a transcendent realm, Joe continued, "He asked me to [put them on you]." It dawned on me that the benevolent, grandfatherly Indigenous presence that had been acknowledged before by others may have been readily sensed in ordinary awareness by Joe. I was again taken aback, caught on my heels. This was either a sophisticated ruse or a legitimate sensing of very subtle energies by one who "sees" deeply. Though I'm not entirely certain, in light of the growing body of coincidences (or synchronicities) it seemed to be the latter.

As someone who wishes to support Indigenous peoples in their healing, hearing comments like "Native American warrior," "beautiful Indian man," "father," or "old man," or being asked to sing Indigenous songs by Indigenous people, has touched me profoundly. These moments seem like an outward validation of something deep within (or moving through) me that seems both impossible, even irrational, and yet intuitively true. Is it possible that I—that we— have had past lives? If so, do we have a soul, spirit, essence, or unique energetic signature that somehow makes its way through time and space to inhabit different bodies?

Despite an absence of objective evidence (in my case at least), I am inclined to think I have Indigenous roots somewhere in my past, and I am indebted to Indigenous Elders for this insight. In fact, on multiple occasions, different Indigenous Elders have pointed out the ways in which myself and other settlers all have some form of Indigenous ancestry. An Elder from a Sundance, Pete Duncan from the Nlaka'pamux Nation, cited Stonehenge as an ancient example of my ancestors' use of similar sacred geometry and transcendent rite to connect with a higher power. Wilfred Gordon, an Aboriginal Elder from the Guugu Yimithirr Nation near Cooktown, Australia, through Socratic questions led a group of settlers to conclude that we are all Indigenous. Shane Pointe, a Coast Salish Knowledge Keeper who lives in present-day Vancouver, said we settlers ought to—need to—connect with our own ancestry. He added that we should not pity local First Nations because they had been colonized for only 150 years, whereas we, the European settlers, had been colonized for two thousand years. Rarely had my perspective shifted so instantly and drastically. These teachings reaffirmed that we are all Indigenous to this planet. How far back do I need to go to connect with my own Indigeneity? Is it but a few generations to a previous life, as the presence of the benevolent Indigenous presence might suggest, or is it two thousand years or more, as I trace my bloodlines from north-western Europe back to my Celtic and Gaul ancestors who lived for millennia prior to Roman invasions of their ancestral homelands.

* * *

I have received so very much from working with my clients. I have developed more insight and acceptance of people. My wife tells me I live more in alignment with the expression "Don't judge a person until you've walked a mile in their shoes." Well, at least, most of the time. Through supporting Indigenous peoples and practicing their traditions, I have felt seen and at home—I experienced a sense of belonging. Contrary to Western mainstream culture's emphasis on individuality, so-called rational or objective knowledge, and material-ism, I have been learning the importance of ancestry, community, and reverence. I am developing sensitivity and insight into the impacts of settler colonialism on both Indigenous peoples and the land itself (in Canada and the world over) and into the resiliency derived from culture and community. I have processed intergenerational trauma of my own and have come to understand that we are all Indigenous. It has dawned on me that life continues to present opportunities for growth, ones that challenge me to face my self-limiting beliefs and judgments, and to humbly share my gifts.

With that said, I have turned away from the path of supporting Indigenous peoples many times. Unhelpful thoughts have badgered me: *It's not my place. You're an imposter. How can I support them when my very settler appearance can be a trigger?* In the long shadow of our peoples' shared, complicated history, we need to find a way to move forward in a good way.

In keeping with the Indigenous Medicine Wheel, which symbolizes fundamental values, the lifespan, nature relatedness, and the four peoples (Black, Red, Yellow, White), a vision came to me to *bring together* the healing traditions of the four peoples to *heal* the four peoples. When the vision came, I was comfortably reclined against a wall in a rustic gathering place with over a dozen others. With eyes closed, I felt transported by music that was mysterious, exotic, and familiar all at once. Unbidden imagery arose and washed over me, sometimes seamlessly pinwheeling from one theme to another without apparent rhyme or reason. Dream-like, this cascade of imagery occasionally paused, as if on cue, to signal that the present image required my attention to explore and uncover some important insight. In one such moment, the top of a mountain appeared beneath me, with my vantage point being in the sky above. Surrounded by other, smaller mountains, this mountain had at its centre an enormous circular caldera filled with red-hot, bubbling lava. Around the periphery of the caldera, in each of the four directions, people were huddled around flags that each bore a symbol representing their beliefs. Within each of these huddles, people clung together in a way that suggested not only uniformity in their beliefs, but also a wariness of those in the other huddles. When viewed on a mountain that eclipsed all others and exuded powerful aliveness in its bubbling lava, these small huddles seemed fearful, misguided, and disconnected from the truth. The image then zoomed out to be viewed in its entirety and from a greater distance. It now conveyed an urgent need for the huddles to set aside perceived differences and come together on the basis of their similarities, to work together in a way that honours all of the peoples and the aliveness and natural laws of the ground beneath all of our feet.

As I sat with this vision, its relationship to the Medicine Wheel (and each of the four peoples) became apparent. Each people possess a rich repository of ancestral wisdom and/or modern technologies that promote health and wellbeing, and we have much to learn from each other. Much as the Medicine Wheel refers to only four peoples (which may seem to oversimplify human diversity), inclusion is central to its design, in keeping with the core belief of "We are all related." This limitation aside, the offerings of these four aggregated peoples are considerable. The Yellow people have shared Taoism, Confucianism, Traditional Chinese Medicine, tai chi, qigong, and Ayurveda, to name but a few. The Black people's wisdom includes shamanism, the importance of nature, herbalism, ritual, community (e.g., Ubuntu, which translates to *I need other human beings in order to be fully human*), and spiritualism. The Red people bring teachings related to traditional diet, herbal remedies, nature relatedness, spirituality, honouring ancestors, plant medicine wisdom, community ceremonies and prayers, and symbolism (e.g., harmony, balance). The White people have brought allopathic medicine, the scientific method, modern technology (via centuries of global trade), Christianity, and, long ago, ritual dance and chanting. When considered together, an astounding collection of wisdom and technology is apparent. This collection is not only a nod to similarity, diversity, and the bio-psycho-social-spiritual conceptual framework, but when integrated in treatment it has the potential to create a powerful healing synergy. Harkening back to the Indigenous Medicine Wheel, its circle shape brings each of its quadrants, which are distinct and interrelated, into direct contact with all of the others. Insofar as each quadrant represents one of the four peoples and their healing practices, the circle shape is an apt visual symbol of integration and holistic health care.

Consistent with this vision, I was once participating in a group with a Blackfoot Elder who had witnessed the crafting of "A Message from Hopi & Other Indigenous Elders." This prophecy is meant to remind us that we are, at this time, surrounded by opportunities to come together and make meaningful change. The assistant shared the prophecy in the appendix of a booklet he had crafted. The prophecy is as follows:

> *"You have been telling the people that this is the*
> *Eleventh Hour. Now you must go back and tell the people*
> *that this is the Hour and there are things to be considered …*
>
> *Where are you living?*
> *What are you doing?*
> *What are your relationships?*
> *Are you in right relation?*
> *Where is your water?*
>
> *Know your garden.*
> *It is time to speak your truth.*
> *Create your community.*
> *Be good to each other.*
> *And do not look outside yourself for the leader.*
>
> *This could be a good time!*
> *There is a river flowing now very fast.*
> *It is so great and swift that*
> *there are those who will be afraid.*
>
> *They will try to hold on to the shore.*
> *They will feel they are being torn apart*
> *and they will suffer greatly.*

Know the river has its destination.
The elders say we must let go of the shore,
and push off into the river,
keep our eyes open, and our heads above the water.

See who is in there with you and celebrate.
At this time in history, we are to
take nothing personally, least of all ourselves.
For the moment that we do,
our spiritual growth and journey comes to a halt.

The time of the lone wolf is over.
Gather yourselves!
Banish the word 'struggle' from
your attitude and vocabulary.
All that you do now
must be done in a sacred manner and in celebration.

We are the ones we have been waiting for …"

"The time of the lone wolf is over." As such, we can only exist as human beings in relation to others. When I shared the vision that had come to me with Cree Elder Mechuskosis, without missing a beat he said, "Oh yeah, I've had that vision too."

About Dr. Rick Miners

Dr. Rick Miners, PhD, is a Registered Psychologist who works in private practice, where he works with children, youth, and adults with developmental, learning, emotional, and behavioural challenges. Across multiple settings, he provides family therapy, consultation to schools, executive coaching, supervision (of early career psychologists), and team leadership. Previously, he conducted research on mindfulness, led mindfulness-based stress reduction programs, and has served as a university lecturer, an organizational health facilitator, and a structural engineer. He was also a sub-investigator and research therapist with the Multidisciplinary Association for Psychedelic Studies' international multi-site MDMA-PTSD treatment study. Rick works from an integrative perspective, drawing primarily from Satir Transformational Systemic Therapy, mindfulness-based, cognitive behavioural, and Indigenous Focusing-Oriented Therapy for Complex Trauma approaches. He has experience with Indigenous healing rites and formal training in psychedelic psychotherapy and has been a therapist for over twenty years.

www.linkedin.com/in/rick-miners-7923171